To Joe Bayly
for making us think

WILLIAM L. COLEMAN is becoming increasingly well known as a gifted writer and author. His specialty has been devotional books for families, which have become bestsellers.

Coleman is a graduate of the Washington Bible College is Washington, D.C., and Grace Theological Seminary in Winona Lake, Indiana. He has pastored three churches and is presently a full-time writer. His articles have appeared in several well-known evangelical magazines. Bill, his wife and three children make their home in Aurora, Nebraska.

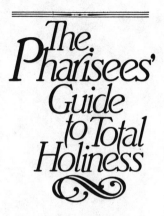

The Pharisees' Guide to Total Holiness

William L. Coleman

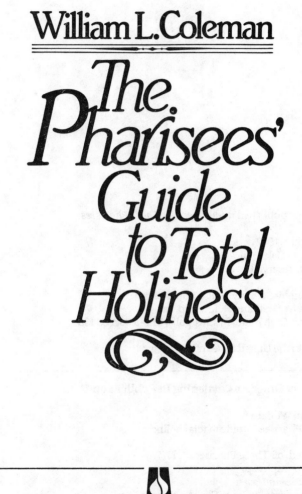

The Pharisees' Guide to Total Holiness

BETHANY HOUSE PUBLISHERS
MINNEAPOLIS, MINNESOTA 55438
A Division of Bethany Fellowship, Inc.

Originally published under the title: *Those Pharisees*

Copyright © 1977
William L. Coleman
All rights reserved

Published by Bethany House Publishers
A Division of Bethany Fellowship, Inc.
6820 Auto Club Road, Minneapolis, Minnesota 55438

Printed in the United States of America

Library of Congress Cataloging in Publication Data

Coleman, William L.
  The Pharisees' guide to total holiness

  Rev. ed. of: Those Pharisees. c1977.
  Bibliography: p.
  Includes index.
  1. Pharisees. 2. Jesus Christ—Attitude
toward Pharisees. I. Title.
BM175.P4C64 1982   296.8'12   82-4551
ISBN O-87123-472-6   AACR2

Acknowledgments

This treatise would have been impossible without the generous cooperation of many people and accompanying institutions. Allow me to thank only a few: the staff at the Aurora City Library—Mrs. Doris Newberry, Mrs. Betty Penner, and Mrs. Mary Griess; the libraries of Hastings College and York College, the Grand Island Public Library, and the excellent Nebraska Inter-Library Loan System; Mrs. Lois Janzen for typing strange markings into legible form and obscure spellings into acceptable English; and William Gentz of Hawthorn Books for superb suggestions

I would also like to thank the Tyndale House Publishers for permission to quote *The Living Bible* and the New York International Bible Society for verses from *New International Version*, Copyright © New York International Bible Society, 1973.

Contents

Introduction:
Prying at a Paradox

The Pharisees are one of the most fascinating groups of people ever to leave their mark on mankind. Part of their excitement comes because they are complicated and mysterious, and yet the paradox is that they are also common, just like the man on today's Main Street.

There are a lot of good reasons to study this ancient fraternity. Their behavior and beliefs tell us a good deal about religion in general. They teach a tremendous amount about the ministry of Jesus Christ. And maybe even more important than these, they give us a chance to look at ourselves. They supply the mirror that will cause us to laugh at our own reflection, and then at the next glance we may want to cry.

Let the reader beware, because if he is anything like the author, he will be tempted to pick out a contemporary group and say, "Aha! These are the modern Pharisees." It is a fool's sport at best. There is in fact no group today that is identical to the Pharisees. Some very accomplished scholars refer to the Pharisees as the "conservatives" of their day. Other equally capable authorities label them as the "liberals."

Because of that fruitless game nothing is accomplished except a bit of second-grade name-calling. The facts seem to bear out that there is a little Pharisee in me and a little Pharisee in you. We are people and not categories, and the real growth comes in our lives as we mature individually.

For most Sunday school–educated and church-nurtured individuals, the very word *Pharisee* conjures up visions of horror akin to the Frankenstein monster or baby snatchers. Be prepared to have some of your prejudices jarred. There were many great and noble Pharisees, as a careful reading of the New Testament will verify. In fact, after studying them, it is easy to see why many practicing Jews still treat the title with respect and honor. Christians need to hear more of the excellent contributions made by an organization that at times excelled in courage and character.

Most Gentiles know something about the suffering that the Jews have encountered. However, most of us know about only the fringes of centuries of torture, persecution, and murder that these people have met. Much of this abuse has come at the hands of professing churchmen. Hopefully every reader will be reminded that Paul was a Pharisee and that Jesus was also a Jew who loved his people.

Every author has his prejudices, and I recognize some of mine. I ~~assume~~ know that the New Testament is accurate and its stories are true. I also ~~assume~~ know that Jesus Christ was correct in his appraisal of the situation. Those who do not agree with these suppositions will have to read the volume more cautiously.

I have felt a need for this type of book for some years. We Christians are frequently discussing and denouncing a group whom we very barely understand. Hopefully this book will bring us a half step closer to a people who had a zeal for God.

A good book is like a good friend. It should make one feel better just to be around it. It should be fine company, stimulate the mind, and jolt the spirit. Don't be afraid to argue with it; don't be reluctant to challenge it; and by all means don't hesitate to ask embarrassing questions. Walk with it in the park, sit with it in the living room, and then ask it to help by explaining which attitudes are dangerously Pharisaic.

1
Pharisaic Fences

A man stood erect and proudly announced, "I am a Pharisee, the son of a Pharisee. I stand on trial because of my hope in the resurrection of the dead."

Those were the bold words of Paul, the most famous of all Christian apostles, as he faced a hostile court of the Sanhedrin. Far from embarrassed by his membership in the group, he appreciated the tough fiber and strict training that he had collected from years in this fraternity.

The Pharisees had given Paul a rock-hard dedication to the laws of God; they had given him a relentless religious zeal, and they had taught him the discipline of discipleship. The apostle carried much of this thorough training into his Christian mission.

It would be impossible to estimate how many such men Pharisaism prepared for the rigors of life. Over the centuries they functioned as the "marine corps" of Judaism, while their dedication and firmness attracted thousands of young men from all over Jewry.

We have been mistaken if we have imagined the Pharisees as a collection of inept buffoons stumbling over each other like a herd of angry Mack Sennett cops. They operated as a highly sophisticated assembly of men who believed they were doing the most important things in all of life. Indeed for some of them this very sincerity tilted them until they could no longer see the world squarely.

It would also be unfair to try to reduce the Pharisees to a simple definition. To blithely declare that they were "hypocrites" or "unloving" or "fanatics" fails to see their complexity and depth. The New Testament, unable to describe the group in a phrase, paints them in myriads of colors.

Just how they earned the name Pharisee is still uncertain. It means "separated ones"; and while it describes an important side of them, it is unclear whether the name came from their friends or their enemies, whether its intention was admiration or mocking.

They could wear the title well since they prided themselves in their denunciation of impure and ungodly elements. Physical separation was of paramount importance. Functional holiness was considered evidence of personal piety, and Lev. 11:44-45 was a central passage.

Their detractors were also happy to use the term but only as a burlesque wit. They considered the Pharisees as a bunch of holy freaks too pious to touch the common man. To them Pharisaism represented a flock of self-righteous prigs.

Whatever the origin of the title, they wore it as did Paul, with dignity. They considered their priorities close to the heart of God.

The Pharisees had no greater task than to protect and propagate the laws of God. Their methods for accomplishing this may seem to be strange and yet, at the same time, may tell us something about ourselves. The zeal to respect and follow the scriptures has led people to do odd things—things that they never saw as radical or unusual.

There is a club that meets regularly, and each time they open their session with a very funny practice. However, not everyone laughs at the practice. In fact you can always tell who is new at the club. The newcomers are fighting back a giggle, but those who have been around awhile don't see anything humorous about it. They have done it so long, they no longer see its humor.

The Pharisaic mentality may have been conditioned the same way. They had so much respect for the original set of scriptures and wanted to protect them so desperately that they started adding to them. Then, after a while, it not only seemed helpful to make additions but absolutely essential. When Jesus began his ministry, he saw these new laws as absurd. Yet the Pharisees saw nothing odd in the practice. They had been doing it a long time.

A college chaplain once suggested that the most serious problem with the Pharisees was that they were basically afraid of God. As ridiculous as this may sound at first, it may come dangerously close to the heart of the matter.

The Pharisees were desperately determined to not break the laws of God. Consequently they devised a system to keep them from even coming close to angering God. They contrived a "fence" of Pharisaic rules that, if man would keep them, would guarantee a safe distance between himself and the laws of God. Therefore, if God said we could not work on the Sabbath, then don't even pick grain to eat, just to play it safe. Don't even heal people because that might be a borderline case.

These laws became known as the *seyag* ("fence"), and they felt they had a biblical command to declare this.[1] The term has also been used by the Scotch Presbyterians. Before they serve the Lord's Supper, they explain who should not partake, and this was called "fencing the table."

The "fence" or "hedge" laws accumulated into hundreds

---

1. George Foot Moore, *Judaism*, vol. 1 (Cambridge, Mass.: Harvard University Press, 1966), p. 259.

over the years and were passed around orally. Soon it became apparent that they were far from optional. These laws became every inch as important as the scriptural laws and in some instances far more crucial.

Their counterpart exists today among people who are afraid to allow Christians to live with God. Our fences are so old and fixed that we too no longer see them, and we even believe they are part of the scriptures themselves. Sometimes we are so afraid that Genesis 1 will be violated that we build a fence and insist that evolution be neither discussed nor studied. Many of us who do not agree with evolution think that if we silence the subject from a distance we can better protect the scriptures. It breathes of insecurity.

Others of us are so distrustful of writers and books that challenge our thinking that we refuse to read anything except that written by our own supporters. We need to keep a safe buffer just in case we cannot stand.

The questions of sexual morality become just as fragile. If we dance, who knows where it might lead? Back up two steps and build a fence. Some movies could corrupt—two more steps back and build another fence. Who knows where wine at mealtime might lead? More fence.

Eventually we are no longer wrestling with the core problems of drunkenness and adultery. Rather we are fighting mock battles at the new fences we have erected. Now the new laws become the really important battlegrounds. Soon we will test a person's orthodoxy by his respect for the fences.

Some will object and say such things have not happened to Christianity. Or have the fences been around so long that we now confuse them with the Bible itself?

The Pharisees would sit very wide-eyed and open-faced and say, "What is wrong with these laws? They are a big help." Jesus replied in essence, "Don't bug me with these little pests. There are more important matters in life."

The group was happy to exercise more flexibility than

merely building walls. They also saw their mission as creating new laws as the times changed. If they felt the Scriptures contained no moral laws to control something modern, then they would manufacture a law and announce that it was henceforth binding on man and God. New situations could not be ignored, and if there were gaps in the Scriptures, someone had to fill them.

These new laws were called gezerah (pl. gezerot), and the term was often used interchangeably with the "fence" laws. Again, these measures seemed perfectly logical, and the practice was based on passages such as Deut. 17:9, "To the priests and Levites, and the chief judge on duty at the time will make the decisions." This left the decisions to contemporaries rather than having to abide by decisions made centuries ago. Economics change, political powers are removed, social pressures are altered. They reasoned that laws must change with them.

While there is sound reasoning to this approach in social and civil laws, if the laws came from God, it became an entirely different matter. Jesus found it very difficult to appreciate a human being's changing God's laws. For him, it was fine if the Pharisees wanted to fast twice a week. They could go to it with great pleasure. The flak came when they said, "We instituted this new law, and God expects you to keep it." At this point Jesus balked and invited them to back off.

Some of them felt that any modern judge was as capable as Moses or Aaron had been in their day.[2] Even if this assumption is valid, however, the crucial point came when they transferred the laws and said God would back them up.

To be certain, Jesus was not the only person to object to

2. Morris Adler, *The World of the Talmud* (New York: Schocken Books, 1966), p. 31.

this practice. Many Jews ignored the gezerot, and some Pharisees were openly critical of their demanding brothers. A local rabbi might proclaim a particular law only to have the general populace treat it with disdain. However, those laws that were accepted by the majority of the Pharisees became as tough as nails.

They seem, in some respects, to resemble the local mores found throughout the United States. In some areas the pastor and congregation come down heavily on mixed swimming, while people in other locals consider such a thing nonsense. Shooting pool used to be frowned on in one region and thoroughly enjoyed in the next. This made it particularly difficult for a traveling missionary to discover what was acceptable in the area he was visiting. (Many missionaries have this problem to this day.)

If necessary, the Pharisees might issue a gezerah that contradicted the biblical command if they felt the situation justified it. Later they might pass another gezerah that would nullify a previous one, but this was understood to be a practical necessity.

They also saw the need for flexibility in different areas and during different eras. Consequently raising cattle might be acceptable for one people and strictly forbidden for another.

In fairness to the Pharisees, their difficulties were not born out of indifference. They cared a lot and gave it their all. However, their very zeal was eating them up and affecting their judgment. They were in fact injuring the possibility of the very close walk with God that they were trying to promote.

The contrast between Jesus and the Pharisees over these laws is seen in no place better than concerning the washing of hands. (We will discuss this incident at length later.)

"Then some of the Pharisees and teachers of the law came to Jesus from Jerusalem and asked, 'Why do your disciples break the tradition of the elders? They don't wash their hands before they eat.'

"Jesus replied, 'And why do you break the command of God for the sake of your traditions?' " (Matt. 15:1–3).

It is this offish attitude that tended to make certain Pharisees unteachable and cast a route of irreconcilable collision between them and Jesus Christ. He reserved his most scathing insults for this group within the group. They knew it all, made themselves the personal authorities over God's guidance.

Of all the degrading titles that Jesus used to describe the Pharisees, none was more devastating then referring to them as "yeast" or "leaven." Before a crowd of thousands, Jesus took on and denounced the most powerful religious machine in Palestine. He told his disciples, "Be on your guard against the yeast of the Pharisees, which is hypocrisy" (Luke 12:1).

The first-century Jewish ear heard something entirely different than we do when someone says *yeast*. To us, it is an additive that causes dough to rise before we bake our bread. To the Jew, it was almost always a sign of impurity and alloy.

The ancient Jews fermented their dough by taking a piece of yeast from a previous baking. They then would knead it into the new dough and try to keep it going. Though they used leaven for their goods, they considered it second best, because unleavened bread had played a special part in their history.

When the Israelites left Egypt, they moved so quickly that they didn't take time to prepare leavened bread. Consequently as they moved about, they ate the unleavened and were glad to have it. In the years to come they celebrated that deliverance (called the Passover) by eating unleavened bread just so they would not forget the hardship and their miraculous escape.

If a Jew would mix yeast into his baking during one of the

annual festivals, the food would be an unacceptable desecration. Christ's audiences understood this principle, and his words didn't fall on deaf ears. When he said the Pharisees were yeast, they knew a heavy insult when they heard one. He was saying that they were corruptive and yet their teachings were being kneaded into Israel until their foulness permeated it all. Not exactly words aimed at pacifying or endearing stiff Pharisees.

However, it is an interesting aside in the New Testament that while the analogy was not lost on the Pharisees, Christ's disciples were completely befuddled by the remark. They looked at each other and said, "It is because we didn't bring any bread" (Matt. 16:7). But then, like many of us, they too often had difficulty separating the figurative and the literal.

Throughout the New Testament leaven is used to describe corruption, with the possible exception of the parable of the leaven in Matt. 13:33 and Luke 13:20-21. Paul used the term to discuss the moral laxity at the church of Corinth and his concern that a little leaven leaveneth the whole lump (1 Cor. 5:6-8).

Part of the wonder of the yeast was in the fact that it was invisible and that it permeated the entire batch. Christ knew that the Pharisees could look very respectable and even helpful while at the same time rotting the very people who admired them the most. One can sense Jesus' frustrations when his disciples think he is discussing bread. Have ears become so dense and hearts become so sedate that they don't see the subtle but thorough diffusion of decay?

Aware of their discussion, Jesus asked them, "Why are you telling about bread? Do you still not see or understand? Are your hearts hardened? Do you have eyes but fail to see, and ears but fail to hear?" (Mark 8:17,18).

It is just as easy for the modern believer to become blind to the gangrene that has spread throughout the church which is sometimes filled with teachings and traditions of purely human origin but that have over the years become so ingrained that they now appear to be of divine origin. Not that there is anything wrong with traditional practices or even with a church's local distinction. However, there is something desperately wrong with presenting these personal preferences as eternal truth.

It must be confusing for the young person to have been taught that the Bible says women should not work out of the home and then in a few years see a deacon's wife working in the local department store. How perplexing it has been to hear identified as the Anti-Christ such names as the Kaiser, Hitler, Mussolini, Kennedy, Kissinger; and then to watch them pass from the scene without eschatological catastrophe. In the process, the faith of Jesus Christ suffers from ambitious but corruptive teaching that was delivered as the very word of God.

Christ's concern over the Pharisees centered around the fact that their opinions, both casual and official, were becoming inseparable with the laws of Moses, and Jesus considered the confusion reprehensible. Let them list their rules and pet practices and label them as "The Forty Favorite Foundations of Pharisaism." More power to them. But do not publish them as the voice of God or as binding on their religious and moral lives.

Maybe Jesus was calling us back to a simple but personal faith that could be shared with the community of other believers. Yet, a faith that is not oppressed or controlled by the group around us.

Not all Pharisaism suffered from a Big Daddy complex. In fact many of them sought a humble, helpful, and satisfying life that walked close to God. However, as is often the case, the most radical extremists of the fraternity were also the most vocal and demanding.

Almost forty years ago Erich Fromm wrote an excellent book called *Escape from Freedom*, which has been reprinted over twenty times. Somewhat critical of the Christian position, it nevertheless raises some serious questions that should be applied to the oppressive Pharisaism.

Fromm concludes that many people are basically afraid of freedom. We find it difficult to make decisions and we actually look for someone to tell us what to do. This "father" offers us a certain amount of security.

Fortunately for Christians, Jesus supplies some of that need by directing our lives. However, the real problem arises when Christ then hands us back a great deal of our freedom. He lets us decide about everyday life, such as entertainment, investments, avenues of service, forms of worship, selecting clothes and friends, and personal habits. Yet inwardly many of us are disappointed. We have agreed to follow Christ, and now we discover that we still have to make decisions.

Freedom becomes frightening again. Rather than learning to enjoy this new liberty, our fear sends us running toward someone who will tell us what to do and maybe even accept a little of our responsibility. Fortunately or unfortunately, there is always someone waiting like a religious con man to take us in. Maybe he is a pastor or a Sunday-school teacher or a Bible-study guide or a personal friend. He will be happy to divide all of life into neat compartments.

He will label this as a sin, that as righteous, the other as godless. He only has two crayons: black and white. He has never owned a gray. He is generous with his decisions and sees his very role in life as dispensing opinions like a candy machine.

He supplies the same contraband the Pharisees produced. He offers instant solutions for people who are afraid of freedom.

This distinction is essential to any discussion of the Pharisees. It is easy to assume that people want to be free from Pharisaism and that great hordes are merely waiting to be taught correctly. Indeed, the very opposite may be the case. While most Christians abhor the name Pharisee, in essence they want very much what the fraternity had to offer. They want someone to build fences so that they will know exactly where to stop. They want to be fenced in so that freedom will not upset them.

For everyone who wants to be a moral slave there seems to be two masters ready to take him. Yet, for those who want one master who will give them tremendous genuine freedom, Jesus Christ offers an alternative.

Among many Christians, freedom and liberty have become dirty words, but to Paul they were symbols of unshackled hearts and lives. "It is for freedom that Christ has set us free. Stand firm, then, and do not let yourselves be burdened again by a yoke of slavery" (Gal. 5:1).

God has given us moral direction that does not need Pharisaic fences.

Questions for Further Thought

1. How would you describe Paul's attitude toward Pharisaism?
2. Can you think of modern religious fences?
3. Are some fences necessary? Explain.
4. What is the difference between a fence and a gezerah?
5. What was the Israelite attitude toward leaven?
6. How did the disciples misunderstand Christ's use of the term *leaven*?
7. Do any Christians you know want non-Biblical fences? Explain.

2
Their Golden Age

No one is able to pinpoint the day and the hour when the Pharisees officially began. Originally they did not gather as a group of businessmen in a hotel in Jerusalem and decided to inaugurate a fraternity. Rather, they came into existence almost spontaneously in answer to a desperate need. They started as a spirit with a noble cause, during the time of the Babylonian exile.

The Jewish people have lived with persecution and exile for most of their history. Seven hundred years before Christ, Israel faced another one of those crucial times of oppression. Palestine at that time was in the middle between two giant powers, Egypt and Assyria. The Jews were not as strong as they had been under King David, and they were even split into two little kingdoms. Consequently, when one of the big powers decided to attack Israel, the Jews would fight tenaciously but seldom had a chance.

Finally the Assyrians began to take seriously the job of conquering Israel. The task proved to be very difficult, and over the years their famous kings led the assault. Eventually Sargon was successful against the ten tribes of the north, and according to his records he carried almost 28,000 Israelites away; and the Bible tells us that "None was left but the tribe of Judah only" (2 Kings 17:18).

The people who went into this captivity were not very strong in their faith, and they lacked good leadership. Consequently, as time went by, they adopted the life and religion of the pagan Assyrians, and they never were able or willing to return to their homeland. Men with the spirit of the Pharisees were completely lacking, and there was no one to hold them together. As a result, they lost their identity among their captors.[1]

One hundred years later we see an almost exact repeat of the situation but with an entirely different outcome. By 600 B.C. the notorious Nebuchadnezzar and his Babylonians had overthrown the Assyrian Empire. The new king thought the time was ripe to pluck Judah, the last apple of Israel.

Nebuchadnezzer tried to make them a tributary that would serve him, but the venture was very unsuccessful. Consequently, over a period of fifteen years he deported practically all of the inhabitants of Judah and its capital, Jerusalem. The Babylonians also stripped the gold from the palace and the temple and sacked all of the treasuries. They later destroyed the city walls, the homes, and the sacred temple. Only a few lower-class people were left in Israel, and the destruction of the Hebrews seemed to be final.

Effectively this should have marked the end of the Jews as a nation. They had no unifying symbol such as the temple. They had no inspiring leadership because their kings were either dead or imprisoned. They were only scattered, cold ashes to be blown to the far corners of the earth, except that some few men refused to let it happen. Men like Daniel, Shadrach, Meshach, and Abednego, and numerous other un-

---

1. George A. Buttrick, ed., *The Interpreter's Dictionary of the Bible*, vol. 2 (Nashville: Abingdon Press, 1962), p. 1,871.

named Hebrews who were committed to the faith and nationality of Judaism. They were determined that their identity would not be erased as it had been for those who were carried away 100 years before.

The details of their labors are difficult to map out with exactness, but we know roughly what was accomplished. These newly assumed leaders saw their primary task to be the teaching of the scriptures to the young so they would not forget the faith of Israel. In order to accomplish this, the Jewish community organized regular classes for religious instruction. We do not know if they met on Saturdays, if they met openly, or if they met secretly at night at first; but we do know they carried on the work.

If someone had asked a local Babylonian citizen where the nearest synagogue was or where you could find a friendly Pharisee, he would probably think a camel had bumped you too hard. Neither one of these existed then as the institutions we think of today. However, the seeds of both began at this time and were vital assets to the Jewish community.[2]

The Jews lived for seventy years under these very trying circumstances. In the back of their minds and recorded among their prophets was the constant hope that they would return to their homeland. Isaiah wrote about some of the hardship and hope they faced. "In that wonderful day when the Lord gives his people rest from sorrow and fear, from slavery and chains, you will jeer at the king of Babylon and say, 'You bully, you! At last you have what was coming to you' " (Isa. 14:3,4, LB).

The steady work of seven decades finally paid off in B.C. 538, when Cyrus, the king of Persia, released the people of Israel to return to Palestine. Not all of the Jews chose to go back. The land was poor and underdeveloped, and many

2. Ibid., vol. 4, p. 478.

had found a new home, a new life-style, and a new religion (Isa. 46). And yet thousands of Jews said yes. They had dreamed of their restoration, and the dreams were kept alive by those who taught them the law and the prophets. Now it was time to see God fulfill all of those well-rehearsed promises.

The forefathers of Pharisaism sent out a call to get to the basis of the faith and hold tightly to it. They are to be congratulated for holding the remnants of Israel together during some of their darkest hours.[3]

The Pharisees' rise to power reads more like a modern novel than like ancient history. It is the story of raw courage, daring heroics, and a deep dedication to God. It is also the account of assassinations, mass murder, and political plotting. These activities centered around the lives of three kings and one queen. We need to look briefly at their intriguing interactions.

ANTIOCHUS EPIPHANES
(CA. 168 B.C.)

Overwhelming hate had captured the passions of the "Greek Hitler," Antiochus IV, or Antiochus Epiphanes.[4] While neither the first nor the last to do so, he declared a program to annihilate the Jewish religion and completely hellenize Judea. He was willing to back up this plan with force, and consequently he sacked Jerusalem and killed thousands of its citizens. He then offered sacrifices to the Olympian Zeus on the Jewish altar, an act of utter blasphemy to the Israelites.

With their backs to the wall and totally outnumbered, the Jews were then able to bind together and write one of the finest chapters in their outstanding history. Rather than

3. Isidor Singer, ed., *The Jewish Encyclopedia*, vol. 9 (New York: KTAV Publishing House, Inc.), pp. 661f.
4. Carl G. Howie, *The Creative Era* (Richmond: John Knox Press, 1965), p. 46.

capitulate, they organized themselves into guerilla groups and fought undercover. Though often outnumbered by as many as six to one, after much bloodshed they regained their freedom under their famous leader Judas Maccabaeus, in 165 B.C., who is remembered to this day as one of the great heroes of Judaism.

For all of its horror, this vicious war accomplished a great deal toward revitalizing a strong nationalistic and religious pride among the Jews. It is out of this spirit of revival that we see the first official mention of a party named the Pharisees, the "separated ones."

JOHN HYRCANUS
(134–104 B.C.)

As the Pharisees began to solidify their views and their strength, they soon came upon what they considered an intolerable situation. It came in the form of a new ruler named John Hyrcanus. As with all controversial figures, some people thought he was the greatest thing that could happen to Israel. Josephus wrote, "He was esteemed by God worthy of the three greatest privileges, the government of his nation, dignity of the high priesthood, and the gift of prophecy, for God was with him and enabled him to know and foretell the future."[5]

The Pharisees did not share his enthusiasm that the "Golden Boy" had arrived, and they believed that he had no right to be both king and high priest. Their wounds were still fresh from the fight for survival, and they were ready to defend the purity of the faith that their comrades had died to preserve.

The normal agitations between the ruler and the Pharisees flamed into bristling hostility after an infamous banquet sponsored by Hyrcanus. Feeling rather magnanimous, the

5. Josephus, *Antiquities*, trans. William Whiston (Grand Rapids: Kregel Publications, 1969), 13.299.

chief of state asked if anyone present had recommendations on ways to improve the government. A gentleman named Eleazar, a Pharisee, stood and suggested that the best thing Hyrcanus could do for the government would be to resign. Then the stunned audience listened as the bold orator expanded on his thesis. Eleazar explained that since Hyrcanus' mother was a captive of the Greeks, she obviously had been violated, and the king was probably the illegitimate son of a Greek soldier, and resignation would be the only honorable thing to do.

Hyrcanus's reaction to the recommendation was less than exuberant. Since he believed that this view was probably generally held among the Pharisees, he began to build a close relationship with the Sadducees, whose observations were less derogatory.

When the king died, his son Aristobulus secured the throne and ruled only one year. His attitudes toward the Pharisees remained belligerent, and he was not universally mourned.

Upon his death an extremely important character came into the lives of the Pharisees. Aristobulus's wife, Salome Alexandra, became the queen, and she was very friendly to the separated party. Her brother is reported to have been a prominent Pharisee, Simon ben Shatach.[6]

ALEXANDER JANNAEUS
(d. 76 B.C.)

Despite this ray of hope, life was destined to become harder before the "Golden Age" could arrive. Alexandra married Jannaeus, whose love for the Pharisees was practically nonexistent.

Normally Jannaeus spent little time fretting over domestic affairs since his first love was foreign conquest. However, he

6. F. F. Bruce, *Israel and the Nations* (Grand Rapids: Wm. B. Eerdmans Publishing Co., 1963), p. 177.

did manage to be home long enough to enrage the Pharisees and to send Judea into civil war.

His difficulties avalanched during the Feast of the Tabernacle. During the ceremony someone refused to pour the water on the altar and instead dumped it on the ground. The Pharisees in the audience began to pelt Jannaeus with their citrons (fruit resembling a large lemon) and started calling insults. The king responded by calling out the troops and slaughtering large numbers of Jews.

The result of this horrendous display was six years of civil war, with the Pharisees fighting tenaciously against the tyrant. The war was particularly cruel and bloody. Jannaeus called on outside Hellenistic troops to help, and on one occasion arrested eight hundred Jews, slaughtered their wives and children before their eyes, and then crucified the men. The Pharisees called him "Son of a Thracian," or a savage.

SALOME ALEXANDRA
(d. 67 B.C.)

The fate of the Pharisees took a sudden turn upward when Jannaeus was mortally wounded. The story that was spread abroad and still survives to this date is that Jannaeus, while on his deathbed, told his wife, Salome Alexandra, to close ranks and make friends with the Pharisees. Whether this story is fabricated or not, the queen did exactly that and thereby healed the nation.

Salome became very open in her support of the Pharisees, and they developed into a powerful political party during her nine-year reign.[7]

While they enjoyed great prominence during the nine-year "Golden Age," they earned it dearly. Serious threats had been made against Judaism both as a religion and as a nation.

7. Jacob Neusner, *From Politics to Piety* (Englewood Cliffs, N.J.: Prentice-Hall, Inc., 1973), p. 50.

The Pharisees and many of their sympathizers rose up to resist those atrocities, and historians tell us that thousands of them gave their blood fighting for the group's existence.

It may surprise many Christians, but to this day the name Pharisee is a very respected memory among modern Jews. Some feel, and justly so, that the New Testament does not tell the whole story of the Pharisees. These men were heroes and champions of Jewish freedom who "represented the finest tradition of their people and of human morals."[8] Compare this concept to *Webster's New Collegiate Dictionary*, which defines the adjective *Pharisaical* as "marked by hypocritical censorious self-righteousness. Syn. see hypocritical."

It is unfortunate that some of the Pharisees allowed the concepts of God and the law to become very brittle and unloving. Jesus correctly denounced the numerous manmade commandments and traditions that were in violation of the laws of God. However, the Pharisees must also receive their place in history as brave men who gave their lives to help preserve a great people.

As we search the New Testament, we will survey both their strengths and weaknesses and find the Gospels mainly concerned with their deficiencies. However, as we travel let us keep their contributions in mind. The Pharisees had the following good points among many. They:

1 were dedicated national heroes
2 accepted the scriptures as God-given
3 were very careful Old Testament students
4 kept the ceremonial laws
5 emphasized education
6 were fervent evangelists
7 were sacrificing tithers
8 anticipated the Messiah.

8. Dagobert D. Runes, ed., *Concise Dictionary of Judaism* (New York: Philosophical Library, 1959), p. 184.

Some of the Pharisees allowed these good qualities to degenerate into mechanical formalism, and there Jesus drew the line as he does with us today.

Questions for Further Thought

1. What was the religious situation in Israel before the captivity?
2. Why did the first group of captives lose their Jewish faith and identity?
3. How may the synagogue have begun?
4. How did the forefathers of Pharisaism prepare for the restoration?
5. In your opinion, what would happen to present-day Christians if our buildings, tax exemptions, national holidays, and salaried ministers were removed?
6. What are some of the enviable strengths of the Pharisees?
7. If the Pharisees are so good, why did Christ speak against them so harshly?

3
Meeting Jesus and John

When Christ was alive on earth, only the Roman government was more powerful in Palestine than the organized and dreaded Pharisees. Because of their prominence it is nearly impossible to appreciate the significance of the ministry of the Nazarene without understanding the strength and mentality of this "community" within the community.

It is estimated that the population of the city of Jerusalem at that time was approximately 25,000 to 30,000. Josephus declares that there were 6,000 Pharisees then living in the same vicinity, which means that more than one out of every ten Jews in Palestine was a Pharisee. Even the Jews who did not belong to this fraternity admired them because Pharisaism was more than a "lodge," it was a set of values and a way of life. They were able to spread their philosophy through the 480 synagogues that dotted the countryside.

The Pharisees were not the only religious fraternity in the area of Jerusalem; they were merely the most influential. There also existed the Sadducees, the Essenes, the "Sons of the Synagogue" and many more, very much like our present societies.

It would be unfair to them if we lumped all six thousand

into one category and assumed that all were alike. Just as in most groups, some were sincere and kind while others were brash, demanding, and unfair. Because there were so many and because they spanned such a large period of time, we find them being described on different occasions in entirely opposite ways.

Rather than austere and formal as we often imagine them, they are referred to in one writing (the *Assumption of Moses*, written during the first century A.D.) as men who "at every hour of the day love to banquet and gorge themselves"; from "morning till evening love to say: we want feasts and plenty to eat." [1]

Part of the reason for the vast variety in Pharisaism is the fact that there were several different branches within the philosophy. Two of the more famous brands were Hillel and Shammai. Some observers feel that Christ did not get along with the Pharisees because most of his dealings were with these two fanatical schools.

The society consisted of numerous educated and professional people such as scribes and priests, including the famous Gamaliel and Paul. However, the great majority consisted of laymen who were carpenters, fishermen, storekeepers. Their leadership may have been sophisticated, but their strength and following was basically grass roots. One author calls them the "people's party." [2]

The Pharisees were not an open group, and several steps were necessary before one could join. Some were accepted after only one month's probation, while others had to wait as long as a year. The historian Josephus tells us that he became a Pharisee at the age of nineteen but had also applied for

1. Joachim Jeremias, *Jerusalem in the Time of Jesus* (Philadelphia: Fortress Press, 1969), p. 250.
2. Norval Geldenhuys, *Commentary on the Gospel of Luke*, The New International Commentary on the New Testament, ed. F. F. Bruce (Grand Rapids: Wm. B. Eerdmans Publishing Co., 1968), pp. 189f.

membership with the Sadducees and Essenes before aligning with the Pharisees.

Naturally, the six thousand did not belong to one local group, but rather several "societies" were scattered throughout the area. Each group had a leader, or a chief Pharisee, and this may be the type of man Jesus ate with in Luke 14:1. We also know that they had regular meetings and shared a communal meal.

There were four degrees at which one could join the group, depending on what vows one took and what duties were carried out. For instance, a person could enlist as a Neeman, which gave him certain privileges but did not make him a full-fledged Chabher, or associate. The Neeman had the right to do business with other Pharisees, while non-Pharisees were very restricted in the amount of trade they could carry out with the "separated ones."

While the society enjoyed a broad base of support, they were by no means universally admired by Jews. A number of rabbis took free-swinging criticisms at them, and some of the general community refused to take them seriously.

A gentleman named Simon Nathaniel married the granddaughter of an established Pharisee, and Simon freely aired his complaints with the crew. His three major objections were that he resisted their purity-of-food laws, he considered their prayers too rigid, and he thought the length of their prayer too exaggerated to be meaningful.[3]

Consequently Jesus was not the first person to criticize this major religious machine. We know of some who did so openly, and it is probably safe to assume that those who belonged to non-Pharisaic groups engaged in considerable defaming, as all rivals do. However, complaining may be entirely different from causing an open threat to the philosophy

3. Jeremias, op. cit., p. 256.

and the organization. While Herod himself could resist the association, even he feared to resist too severely.

Herod issued an edict that everyone must bow down to the king and to Caesar, and the Pharisees flatly refused. While it is true that Herod fined them for their disobedience, he had other people executed for the same offense. One must conclude that the ruler did not feel fearless or limitless in his authority over this powerful institution.

Members of the fraternity took full advantage of the social and political clout they possessed. In studying them one can almost picture them with a spiritual "strut," moving conspicuously through the community. Many of their religious observances and routines were exaggerated to achieve the maximum public display. Their prayer times would be kept regularly each day whether in public or private. The farmer would put down his hoe, the cobbler would lower his needle, and the merchant would lay aside his cloth; and in full view of everyone they would pray. This exercise would send them bending far over to the ground in extreme effort and pomp in a show that could not be ignored by the man on the street. Indeed, if prayer time found them in the middle of a road, they bowed immediately, and the traffic could wait until the solemn occasion ran its course.

If the group had a key to its philosophy, it could be stated, "How do we look?" They placed extreme emphasis on the question of the external rather than the internal. This is one of the reasons why Jesus locked horns with them so often. His emphasis in life was exactly the opposite. Historians tell us that the core of their vows can be summed up in two areas: (1) tithing and (2) purification. Do we look right rather than are we right. Paul was a Pharisee, and he described the system very well. In Acts, chapter twenty-six, the apostle spoke before King Agrippa, defending himself in light of the uproar by the Jews. Part of his argument was that he was a good Jew. "They have known me for a long time and can testify, if they are willing, that according to the strictest sect of our religion, I lived as a Pharisee" (v.5).

While the Pharisees were dedicated to the written word of the scriptures handed down by Moses and the prophets, they did not consider these as God's sole revelation. They also possessed large amounts of oral traditions and laws. They believed that these were handed down by God and were of equal significance. Christ found these teachings to be unacceptable and refused to subject himself or his disciples to these religious rigors.

Apart from the mechanics and organization of the fraternity two facts affect the life of Christ more than any other. First, the Pharisees were the most powerful religious party of the time. Second, they were the most rigid group, inflexible, unyielding, and intractable.

Consequently, it is a very fair estimate when Jeremias concludes, "It is an act of unparalleled risk which Jesus performed when, from the full power of his consciousness of sovereignty, he openly and fearlessly called these men to repentance, and this act brought him to the cross." [4]

If we were seeking to demonstrate opposites within the Jewish community, no better examples could be found than the Pharisees and John the Baptist. The Pharisees were very much the establishment; they were prestige-conscious, highly organized, and regimented to rules. John was very ascetic, revolutionary, fairly isolated, and independent. When John's message and ministry became popular, a clash with the ruling party was inevitable. These two strong-willed ideologies could not coexist peacefully.

John was probably not a member of the Essenes sect; however, there are some basic similarities between the two. The

4. Ibid., p. 267.

Essenes chose the simple life, including communal living and a preference to avoid marriage. Some of them made their homes in the wilderness to devote themselves to an uncomplicated existence, and they were thoroughgoing Jews. This is what gives rise to the speculation that John was numbered among them, and some feel that even Jesus may have spent time with the group.

However, it is much safer to assume that John was an individual who felt the call of God to be a prophet and who was busily engaged in fulfilling that purpose. Eating honey and locusts while wearing a camel's hair coat may have been unacceptable to the Pharisees but would not of itself incur their wrath. Rather, two things apparently pushed them to the boiling point. First of all, he drew crowds, and this always proved a threat to the established religious leaders. Second, he carried Jewish credentials. The combination warranted close scrutiny from the fraternity that considered themselves the guardians of the truth and of "true Israel."

The first confrontation between the two is recorded in John 1:24, with a corresponding passage in Matt. 3:7–9. The preaching of the Baptist centered on three areas: the Messiah, repentance, and water baptism. All three were not only recognizable but of vital importance to the Pharisees. Consequently the Pharisees and the Sadducees made an "official" journey to investigate the evangelist.

John wasn't difficult to find since he hardly operated under a bushel. He used the Jordan River, preached along the countryside, and gave public invitations. We know that the delegation that came to see him was official because the passage in John says they were sent or commissioned. Many scholars feel that the ruling Sanhedrin would not have done this, and in all probability they are representing the Pharisees. However, since Matthew includes the Sadducees, the question of who sent them is open. We do know that a larger, more powerful assembly delegated them, and they arrive with purpose and not merely curiosity.

Being Bible scholars, they are aware that baptism could have great significance to the coming Messiah. Ezekiel predicted that God would sprinkle clean water on Israel and cleanse it from its filthiness (36:25; 37:23). Consequently baptism would be a matter of interest to them.

When they approached John, the Pharisees went directly to the heart of the matter. John had denied publicly that he was the Messiah, Elijah, or the prophet.[5] The Pharisees believed that he was neither of these (partly because they wanted to believe it), and they came to the only logical conclusion: He had no right to baptize and infringe on their religious matters. They asked him, "Why then do you baptize . . . ?" (John 1:25).

John answers the inquiry very concisely and explains that someone else is coming who will baptize with something better than water. He certainly implies the approaching Messiah, which would be of considerable interest to their fraternity.

If we assume that both passages[6] are the same account, we then see John turning on his visitors in a most vicious attack. He denounces them boldly with acid confrontation. He calls them snakes (a term no more flattering then than now) and asks them, probably mockingly, who warned them to flee the coming judgment. It is likely ridicule on the prophet's part since the Pharisees hardly considered themselves in urgent need of conversion.

Rather than welcoming the entourage with pleasure, John became immediately suspicious and hostile. He acknowledges the fact that they are worlds apart and any amenities will only lead to trouble. Consequently he calls a spade a

5. Deut. 18:15–18.
6. John 1:24 and Matt. 3:7–9.

spade so no one will be confused into thinking that he considers the Pharisees the spiritual elite.

Such brash criticism of the super-holy could not go unanswered, and the Pharisees made serious and possibly fatal inroads into the Baptist's ministry. He could not be ignored if he were to persist in accumulating large crowds and in openly irritating "true Israel."

Luke (7:29,30) tells us that John's ministry was having considerable impact: "All the people, even the tax collectors, when they heard Jesus' words, acknowledged that God's way was right, because they had been baptized by John. But the Pharisees and experts in the law rejected God's purpose for themselves, because they had not been baptized by John."

John had gathered a number of disciples in the same manner that Jesus did, and the Pharisees were able to have an influence on them. In Matt. 9:14 we find those disciples asking Jesus why they and the Pharisees fast and the disciples of Jesus do not. Jesus replied that this is not the time to fast since they have reason to be happy.

Under the guidance of the Pharisees, fasting had evolved into a monster during the time of John. During the Old Testament times, fasting was limited to once or twice a year and might otherwise be observed on a private, quiet level. The Pharisees took it from a form of simple worship and developed it into a complex organization surrounded by rules and intimidation. During the time of Jesus, Jews were expected to fast on the second and fifth day of the week and even more frequently if they possessed exceptional piety (Luke 18:12).

The Pharisees must also receive credit for disfiguring fasting. Instead of it becoming a glad form of sacrifice to God, they turned it into a sourpuss sanctity. Christ called them hypocrites, "for they do disfigure their faces to show men they are fasting" (Matt. 6:16). Jesus told them that if they were going to fast, clean up their faces and be cheerful; no one appreciates a grouch for God.

How much of this controlled the thinking of John's disciples we cannot be certain, but there is strong evidence that was considerable. Yet it cannot surprise the reader since the Pharisees had such widespread influence over the religious community that their practices necessarily affected almost everyone.

Nowhere in their practices do we have a clearer picture of something good becoming so thoroughly corrupt. Fasting could have been uplifting and simple for the average believer. Yet by the time the Pharisees had stretched it and added restrictions, it became an awesome responsibility void of meaning because it was shackled with formalism.

We cannot be positive of how far the Pharisees went in their influence on John's life and ministry. It would be very easy, though extremely unfair, to make them worse villains than they really were, but we must avoid taking cheap shots. Nevertheless we also are aware that a lot of maneuvering goes on in history behind the scenes without the public knowing it. With these principles in mind let us consider an observation made by Edersheim.

We are familiar with the facts surrounding the death of John. He criticized Herod Antipas for marrying his brother's wife, and as a result Herod had John arrested. Later Herod promised Salome anything she wanted up to half of his kingdom; and after consulting her mother, the dancer demanded John's head. Though Herod sorely regretted it, he complied and executed the evangelist.

Edersheim, after reading John 4:1,2, concludes correctly that the close scrutiny of the Pharisees caused Jesus to withdraw from Judea to Galilee. The same passage states that John was an equal concern to the Pharisees, but he did not separate himself from the territory. Consequently, Edersheim reasons that pressure from the Pharisees allowed Herod to arrest his adversary without fear of upsetting the "people's party." [7] The theory is interesting and not without merit.

Questions for Further Thought

1. Some describe the Pharisees as kind and others call them unreasonable. Why?
2. Why are they called the "people's party?"
3. How can the Pharisee philosophy best be stated?
4. Are we more concerned with appearances than sincerity? Explain.
5. Why was John the Baptist a threat to the Pharisees?
6. Why did John attack the Pharisees?
7. How can we reconcile John's treatment of the Pharisees with Jesus' teaching to love our enemies?

7. Alfred Edersheim, *The Life and Times of Jesus the Messiah* (Grand Rapids: Wm. B. Eerdmans Publishing Co., 1971), p. 658.

4
Sourpuss Sacrifice

There are few people more boring than the person who brags about the sacrifices he has made; the parent who complains, "After all I have done for you"; or the chairman rehearsing what he has done for the club.

When it comes to worshiping God, the practice of boasting becomes particularly reprehensible. That is why Jesus told the Pharisees (and us) that if fasting causes our face to warp like wet plywood, then we would be better off to just forget about it (Matt. 6:16–18).

Christ's observation on the subject was not earthshaking, because many religious people recognize the fact that worshiping God is basically an internal matter rather than a big show. Knowing it is one thing, but doing it may be an entirely different world.

It is true that the Pharisees understood this principle and taught it to their followers. They said, "He who fast. and makes a display of himself to others, to boast his fasting, is punished for this."[1] However, we must appreciate the fact that there is often an enormous gap between written instruc-

1. Israel Abrahams, *Studies in Pharisaism and the Gospels*, Library of Biblical Studies, ed. Harry Orlinsky (New York: KTAV Publishing House, Inc., 1967), p. 125.

tions and actual practices. The Puritans had strict laws against premarital sex and drunkenness, yet they had difficulties with both unwed mothers and public intoxication.

The Pharisees attempted a conscientious approach to fasting and the devout life. They felt that while some asceticism was helpful, too much of it distorted a person's view of life and God. Consequently, they encouraged people to have a good time, and they considered a reasonable indulgence in life to be a definite asset. In a famous quote in the Talmud, Abba Arika is reported as saying, "On the day of reckoning man will have to give an account of every good which his eyes beheld and which he did not enjoy." [2]

With this open, adventurous attitude, how did the local Pharisees clash with Christ over the matter? To find the solution one must unlock some old doors out of the past and see the route that biblical fasting has taken.

Fasting was definitely a part of the Mosaic system, and Lev. 23:27–29 provides instructions to withdraw from the normal cares and work of life. This became a national day of fasting to celebrate the Day of Atonement. If this passage teaches regulated fasting, then it is certainly the only place where it is commended. All other cases, and there are many, represent fasting as an individual and voluntary practice. Normally it accompanied grief, sin, trying to avoid calamity, or even wrestling for the guidance of God.

However, after the Exile fasting became more prominent among the Jews and far less optional. Five national days of fasting were added to the list, and we find the Jews arguing with the prophet Zechariah as to whether or not they are really necessary (Zech. 7).

By the time Jesus begins his ministry, fasting has turned the corner from being a helpful addition to a life of piety to now becoming, for some, a burdensome badge that proves

2. Ibid., p. 122.

one's righteousness. Fasting began as a practice for once a year, moved to every few months, and for some the first century saw it being practiced no less than twice a week (Luke 18:12).

All of this could have been very innocent, and doubtless much of it was. So much so that several writers feel that Christ was unfair in his criticism of Pharisaic fasting. However, one must pause to ask if Christ has been given a just hearing in this case. Technically speaking, Jesus did not object to the frequency of the fasting. His reservations went deeper, into the attitude and showmanship of their conduct.

Specifically, Christ rebuked three aspects of fasting as he saw it among the Pharisees. It is reasonable to assume that many Pharisees objected also.

First, Christ considered the sourpuss sacrifice as unacceptable to God and to man (Matt. 6:16–17). On days of public fasting it was understandable that fasting might not be accomplished in a closet. However, Christ questioned a believer's intentions when he disfigured his face in order to announce his piety. Christ's advice was to wash our face, slick down our hair, and be cheerful because we are pleased to worship God. To look miserable is not a merit to God or to the local group of believers.

Second, Christ rejected the self-righteous attitude that often traveled with fasting. Sometimes we miss the point of the Pharisee who thanks God in Luke, chapter eighteen. The difficulty is not that he fasted twice a week. Some Pharisees did fast this often,[3] and the Jewish teachers warned against such extremism. Mar Samuel declared the constant faster to be a sinner; to fast too often was believed to make the person unfit for the "work of heaven."[4]

Yet this does not appear to be Christ's complaint. Let them

3. Geldenhuys, op. cit., p. 452.
4. Abrahams, op. cit., p. 126.

fast every other day if they wish to, but do not let them assume that they are righteous because they fast. This man lacked a humble heart before God. This man abused the grace of God. This man believed he had stature with God because he was a chronic faster. This was too much for the Messiah, and he spoke up.

Third, Jesus refused to allow other people to infringe their rules for piety upon him, his disciples, or anyone else. In this, Christ rang another bell for religious liberty (Mark 2:18-20).

Why should he or his disciples fast? They are not sad, repentant, and do not feel estranged from God. The Bridegroom is with them, and they have a great deal to be happy about. Should they fast merely because other people fast? Are the Pharisees and John's disciples so insecure that they must impose their practices on other people?

Christ drew an important line for all believers. He decided to not comply with every religious routine merely to keep everyone happy. That route is the road to stiff formalism rather than individual response.

Bonhoeffer sums up Christ's attitude very well. "Jesus, however, bids his disciples to persevere in the practices of humiliation, but not to force them on other people as a rule or regulation. They must rejoice and give thanks for the privilege of remaining in the service of their Lord." [5]

Wherever Christ saw men and women emphasize laws and deny the spirit, he was careful to point out the futility of it and remind us that we must worship in spirit and in truth.

(In a strange sense the Pharisees may have gotten the last laugh. By the second century A.D. the church had incorporated two fast days per week and maintained it as a regular practice. People are basically the same all over.)

Maybe there are many other aspects of our Christian lives

5. Dietrich Bonhoeffer, *The Cost of Discipleship* (New York: The Macmillan Co., 1973), p. 191.

and worship that have long been dead and thoughtless. With some people it may be the three and four services they attend each week. Sometimes they have become monotonous and lifeless treks that have become meaningless and in some cases even mindless. Yet we go, without stopping to evaluate their relative value or asking what God may think of them.

For others it may be the form of worship, with routines that have not altered appreciably in four hundred years. Maybe they have become exercises in penitence to be endured as punishment from God. Possibly we revel in their dullness, because it speaks well of our piety that we did not enjoy the experience; and one can only guess what God thought of the ceremony.

Christ has taught us that God is not impressed with unconscious worship. Whether it is singing hymns that we do not feel or mean or writing checks that are a dutiful pain rather than a zeal for a heavenly Father.

Jesus challenged them to check out their form of service and worship because it was becoming a disgrace. Would it be beyond him to call us to the same inventory?

We made reference to Zechariah, chapter seven, in which the Jews asked if they could stop fasting now that the Exile was over. His reply runs like an inexhaustible vein of pure gold. God asked them if they were thinking about him as they fasted and then answered his own rhetorical question.

"No, not at all! And even now in your holy feasts to God, you don't think of me, but only of the food and fellowship and fun!" (7:5,6).

On the one hand, worshiping God has become dismal and empty. On the other hand, worshiping has become a meaningless social. In the middle, Christ asks us to worship with sincerity and happiness.

Whenever someone feels that God has appointed him as the moral policeman over the lives of others, he does indeed have a difficult life. The Pharisees were always the best audience that Christ had. They listened to every word he said and took note of each action he made. They were the watchdogs of the religious community; their efforts were endless. Luke tells us that the Pharisees tried to "besiege him with questions, waiting to catch him in something he might say" (11:53).

Their job was made enormously difficult by the large numbers of rules they had to enforce. Not only were they knee-high in Old Testament regulations, but also they were completely smothered by almost countless laws that they themselves added. These additional laws are referred to as the traditions of the fathers or the oral law. The oral laws were originally gracious attempts to help. Since it was difficult to interpret many of the Old Testament laws, these extra laws were added to help clear up the meaning. However, as time went on, the oral laws, finally codified in the Mishnah (ca. A.D. 200), became just as important as the written laws.[6]

It is easy to appreciate the dedication that Christ demonstrated to the laws of Moses. He not only kept them in fact but he also insisted that they be followed in spirit. However, we find him continuously locking horns with the Pharisees over their extra laws. In this aspect Jesus was unyielding. Whether it was healing, picking corn, fasting, or in this case washing hands, the Nazarene refused to back off. In essence he is saying, "If you think I am going to keep all of your picky little religious rules, you have another guess coming." Far from acquiescing to their petty principles in order to keep peace, he turned them down flatly.

Mark 7:1–8 is a classic example of the type of confrontation that often awaited them.[7] The Pharisees had noted the

6. John Bright, *A History of Israel* (Philadelphia: The Westminster Press, 1972), p. 464.
7. Also Matt. 15:2; Luke 11:38.

fact that Jesus' disciples were eating their bread with unclean hands. Obviously, their concern was not one of hygiene, and no one suggests that the disciples were careless at this point. Rather their point of contention was the flagrant violation of their oral traditions.

As with most abuses in life the Pharisees began working with a solid principle. The Old Testament contains extensive laws of purity, and many are explained in Leviticus, chapter fifteen. Some such laws were functional for the actual sake of cleanliness, and others were strictly ceremonial as a symbol of purity. Certainly Eleazar's instructions concerning the cleansing of weapons both by water and fire were basically ceremonial (Num. 31:20–24).

The Pharisees are all for such symbols, and they are even willing to outdo the scriptures. If these cleansings are good, then why not carry them into other areas of life? Consequently, their logic allowed them to leap from the known will of God to the assumed will of God so easily that later they confused the two. Then they began to construct these guides to holy living. Since cleansing by water is an excellent symbol, let us make our lives more holy. Why not have a ceremonial cleansing before each meal? And if that is such a noble step, why not double it and have everyone wash after each meal also? A capital concept; and rules and regulations began to take shape in order to make excellent display of holiness.

"Extremely minute too are the directions concerning the washing or correct pouring upon the hands. It was needful that the hands should always have water poured on them before eating. (To dip them into water was only necessary for eating holy things, i.e., things pertaining to sacrifices.) Then it was fully discussed, from what vessels such pouring should take place, what water was suitable for it, who might pour it, and how far the hands must be poured on." [8]

8. Emil Schürer, *A History of the Jewish Peoples in the Time of Jesus Christ*, vol. 2, div. 2 (New York: Charles Scribner's Sons, 1896), p. 111.

In order to observe this law, people had to keep large supplies of water on hand. The water was kept in sizable jars, and considerable pains were taken to assure its purity. Water was then drawn from the vessels in containers that could not measure less than one and one-half eggshells. From these the water was poured onto both hands as they were lifted into the air. The water was then allowed to run down onto the wrists. If for any reason the water did not reach the wrists, the hands were still officially unclean.

As with all man-made religious laws, both a rationale and a penalty had to be devised in order to keep the practice going. The rationale that was promoted went something like this. We must ceremoniously clean our hands before we eat because it is in keeping with the Old Testament principles and it has sanitary significance. It is also our duty to wash our hands after we eat because if we rub our eyes we might injure them from the bread crumbs, and soldiers could even become inefficient by greasy palms. Consequently, those who aspire to even greater dedication might even consider washing their hands between each course.[9]

Early in their existence these laws left the point of being helpful and recommended and soon joined the ranks of the compulsory. The Pharisees were not upset at Christ because he was hostile to friendly advice. The Pharisees were disturbed and asked, "Why don't your disciples live according to the traditions of the elders instead of eating their food with 'unclean hands'?" (Mark 7:5). They felt that to neglect this practice was to commit a gross carnal defilement. To disregard it was to risk some temporal destruction, such as financial poverty. Even the bread that was eaten was considered little more than filth.

Edersheim tells us that at least one rabbi was excommunicated because he disregarded this imposed ceremonial law. Around A.D. 30 they would like to have punished

9. Edersheim, op. cit., pt. 2, pp. 9ff.

another rabbi, named Jesus, for violating the same law. Creators of religious laws are the same all over and often allow their systems to degenerate into hate machines.

How did this law get started? Who suggested it in the beginning? Since they were unable to trace or justify its origin, some of them tried to paint some dignity on it and claimed that Solomon must have established it someplace.

Jesus made short work of the whole subject. Since they maintained respect for the written law, he quoted one of its writers, Isaiah, "These people honor me with their lips but their hearts are far from me. They worship me in vain; their teachings are but rules made by men" (29:13). Christ refused to be intimidated by the super-holy and drew a conclusion to summarize what they were doing lest they miss the point. "You have let go of the commands of God and are holding on to the traditions of men." Man-made rules masquerading as God's truth are extremely dangerous, and yet they have always been with us. A hundred years ago Dwight L. Moody lamented the sins of men wearing ruffled shirts. At the turn of the century Billy Sunday spoke out boldly against women chewing gum. One backwoods deacon counted it a sin to whistle.

No national crusade will cause such tinkering to go away, but there is freedom for the individual—the same type of freedom Jesus espoused and practiced. Others could make up all of the petty doctrines they wanted, but don't expect Christ to play their game.

What the Pharisees could not appreciate and what we modern editors are blind to is that the Bible is complete. It does not need a revised edition flanked with local laws and mores to keep it contemporary.

Questions for Further Thought

1. How did the practice of fasting evolve?
2. What was Christ's problem with the Pharisee type of fasting?
3. Why did not Christ's disciples fast?
4. Does fasting have a proper use in our present day? If so, what is it?
5. Are there religious functions that have been "sourpuss" sacrifices in your life?
6. What laws do you feel have been added to Christianity in your community?
7. Why do people add to biblical laws?

5
Beware Bigger Bigots

When Jesus looked up into a tree and invited himself to have dinner with a short man named Zacchaeus, he knew what kind of risk he was taking. Tax collectors, not popular in any age, were particularly hated in the first century B.C.

The Romans occupied the land of Palestine, and the Jews found it difficult to enjoy the presence of foreign troops on their soil. As with any government, some system of taxation had to be arranged if the empire was to flourish. Consequently the Romans derived a system to collect poll, land, and tool tax from both friend and foe.

Because the empire was so large, the government sold franchises to "stock companies" of Romans who would in turn collect the local toll tax. That would include toll stations on major roads, at seaports, and at the gates of cities. These "stock companies" would hire men under them, who in turn would hire other men to do the actual collecting. For instance, Zacchaeus was a chief tax collector at Jericho and controlled a local territory, while Matthew-Levi maintained a particular booth.

The system was set up with great flexibility and tremendous room for corruption. The stock companies had to pay a certain amount to the government each year, but how much they collected from the local people was entirely up to the tax officer. By the time everyone raked his share off the top and probably even stole a little, the taxpayer was terribly abused.

The feelings for any Jew who would debase himself into the position of tax collector for the Romans ran the gamut from great appreciation to absolute contempt. It is easy to see both sides. The Roman Cicero referred to tax collectors as "the flower of knighthood," "the ornament of the state," and the "strength of the republic." Obviously, the splendor of Rome could not flourish without these captains of the coffers.

Most of the resident Jews saw them in a shoddy light. The Jews still considered themselves an independent people invaded for a time by another power. Many felt the day would come when they would shed their yoke and be a free nation again.

To these nationalists any Jew who would help Romans collect taxes was a rodent of the worst nature. Then, to add insult to injury, they realized that these "traitors" were getting wealthy at the expense of their oppressed brothers.

The picture becomes clearer if we imagine how the situation was in France during the German occupation of World War II. If some of the Frenchmen had tried to collect taxes to support the Nazis, they would have been hated with intense heat. Men like Zacchaeus are in exactly that position (Luke 19:1–10).

The description we have given the Jewish tax collector already qualifies him as part of the dandruff of the world. However, if we look closer, his role only becomes more sinister. Suppose a local Jew was unable to pay his taxes. Then the publican would accommodate him by loaning him the money at exorbitant interest rates.[1] Consequently the average citizen's financial burdens could become impossible.

1. Alfred Edersheim, *Sketches of Jewish Social Life* (Grand Rapids: Wm. B. Eerdmans Publishing Co., 1964).

If the individual was unable to pay these heavy assessments, he could be treated in the cruelest fashion. He could be grabbed by the throat and hauled off to the local jail. There he could remain and rot until his relatives or friends were able to raise his sum (Matt. 18:28–30).

This brief job description doesn't qualify the tax collector as a candidate for "Mr. Israel," but it is a frank look at a traitor/crook as the Pharisees saw him. It is only natural that the contemporary Jews looked at him with acid viciousness.

The Pharisees and rabbis began to develop a system to exclude the tax collector from all of their activities. They were considered on the same level as professional robbers. They were not allowed to give testimony in a Jewish court. They could not hold any communal office. Any gifts they gave to charities were to be refused. If a Jew was able to lie to a tax collector and get away with it, they considered it an act of righteousness rather than an insult to God.

But suppose the tax collector became convinced of the errors of his ways and decided to repent. He would like to give up his graft and be reunited with God. The rabbis were persuaded that such repentance was impossible. After all, the tax collector had stolen so much money that there was no possible way for him to make restoration.[2] This was altered later.

It is necessary to understand the part publicans played in Israel and the reactions of the Pharisees in order to appreciate the ministry of Jesus Christ. One day, early in his collection of disciples, he stopped beside a tax collector's booth (possibly outside Capernaum) and looked at Matthew-Levi and said "Follow me" (Matt. 9:9). When Matthew stepped out of that shed and accepted the invitation, Christ drove a key nail in his diplomatic coffin. When the

2. B. K. Talmud, *The Interpreter's Dictionary of the Bible*, vol. 4, ed. George A. Buttrick (Nashville: Abingdon Press, 1962), p. 522.

Pharisees knew that Christ ate in the home of the wretched revenuer, it was clearly demonstrated to them that he could not possibly be the Messiah.

Jesus had the option of ignoring the problem and merely treating publicans as part of the crowd. Certainly some of his friends worried about his potential for upsetting the Pharisees (Matt. 15:12). However, Christ possessed a compassion for the tax collector that would not allow him to play games with the religiously prudish.

Tax collectors, for all of their faults, were a spiritually starving people. There was no one to minister to them and demonstrate that they cared. Consequently when Christ opened his love toward them, they responded in droves. Luke tells us that on one occasion "all" of the publicans came to hear Jesus (15:1). Whether we take "all" literally or as a hyperbole, we realize that large numbers came readily.[3] They had reacted in similar manner to the inclusive preaching of John the Baptist as they dotted his audiences (Luke 3:12; 7:29).

Over the centuries of Christian history the exact pattern has proven true repeatedly. Christians who will catapult the bigotry to minister to outcasts often have found them responsive to love and acceptance. The Booths of the Salvation Army found it true among prostitutes. The Moravians found it true among the lepers. Robert Raikes demonstrated it among the poor children of London. Amy Carmichael proved it with the slave girls of the temples in India.

This evident attitude by Jesus adds a lot of light to what he taught us about how to treat our brother when he sins. Christ said to treat him as a "pagan and a tax collector" (Matt. 18:17). How then did Christ treat them? With compassion and with patience. As outsiders who needed help, to

3. A. T. Robertson, *Word Pictures in the New Testament*, vol. 2 (Nashville: Broadman Press, 1930), p. 204.

be sure, but not with disgust or abandonment. He did not share the same approach as the Pharisees, whose pattern it was to despise the spiritually deprived.

Maybe this speaks very directly to our present world. Possibly current Christians have backed away from the social outcast. We may have been so busy condemning the bartender that we forgot to minister to him. Sometimes we have been more intent on running the prostitute off than on offering her hope. Maybe we have denounced those of different religions so loudly that they do not know we love them for all of the din. Christ knew that many would not understand him, but he decided to build a bridge to a needy people anyway.

But what was Christ telling these tools of the Romans? Was he reassuring them that they were doing the right thing? Was he giving them the high sign to keep gouging the Jews? When we look at Zacchaeus, we see that part of Christ's ministry was to correct what they had been doing wrong. After Jesus ate with the "chief publican," the change in that life was obvious. He called Christ "Lord," he gave one-half of his goods to the poor, and whomever he had cheated he repaid fourfold. Christ was then glad to announce, "Today salvation has come to this house" (Luke 19:1–10).

John the Baptist did exactly the same thing. We do the ascetic an injustice by imagining that he played a one-string instrument by merely repeating, "Repent, repent," over and over again. The publicans, with hungry hearts, asked John, "Teacher, what should we do?" And he replied, "Don't collect any more than you are required to" (Luke 3:12).

The Pharisees could not see beyond their immediate national difficulties. They did not think to evaluate the good that Christ was accomplishing. They merely went into a fit. The association of Jesus with publicans automatically disqualified him as any form of a representative of God. Repeatedly they challenged him and his disciples over the puzzle: Why does he eat and mix with publicans? (Matt. 9:11). When they looked for something nasty to call him, they threw in the dual description of wine bibber and friend of publicans (Matt. 11:19).

It would have been more comfortable for Jesus to have sidestepped this issue. After all, people might have argued then as they do now: "Don't make waves." "Protect the unity of the believers." "We can't afford enemies if the people are going to support you." But Christ was too much the Son of God to fall for this type of compromise. He refused to neutralize the power of God by yielding to the pressure of those who were bigoted and inbred.

Just in case the Pharisees might miss his point—and they couldn't—he went one step further to painfully spell it out. He told the story of two men who went to the temple to pray. One man was a Pharisee and the other was a tax collector.

The Pharisee prayed, "God, I thank you that I am not like all other men—robbers, evildoers, adulterers—or even like this tax collector. I fast twice a week and give a tenth of all my income."

Then the tax collector prayed, "God have mercy on me, a sinner."

Then, lest they miss a very obvious point, Jesus said, "I tell you that this man, rather than the other, went home justified before God" (Luke 18:9–14). At this point it had become difficult for the Pharisees to distinguish between confidence and cockiness.

It is one thing to be assured that God is good to us, it is quite another to feel that God made us a little better than others. It is easy to become deluded and believe our church is a little better than any other in town or that our set of beliefs has a corner on God. It is almost amusing to watch the charismatic and the noncharismatic individuals each proudly proclaim their special places.

Christ gave us a lesson that many could not grasp. Because

God has been good to us, we are a humble, grateful people, not a haughty, better class. A lack of humility cost the Pharisees their pliability and prevented them from serving the needy publicans.

When Jesus preached the Sermon on the Mount, he told us to love our enemies; after all, anyone can love those who love in return. Then he said, "Are not even the tax collectors doing that?" And we can almost hear the Pharisees' teeth grinding.

This glaring bigotry also spilled over to nationalities. In this respect they resembled the twentieth-century hate that pours out of ignorance and intolerance. During the first century one of the main objects of their prejudice was against a group called Samaritans. They were a people who lived north of Judea, and the hostility between the two stretches back almost eight hundred years.

Great hordes of Jews were deported during the time of the Assyrian and Babylonian captivities, but some people were left in the land. Foreigners then moved into the area and eventually intermarried with the remaining Jews, and they had children of mixed nationality. Years later, when the exiles returned to Palestine, they refused to accept the "impure" Samaritans.

Consequently we have another classic case of a group of people who cannot stand another class of people because they are different. It is extremely similar in passion to the difficulties that have been encountered by the Philippines and the Chinese, the South African whites and the nationals, the Ethiopians and the Italians, the Protestants and the Catholics in Ireland; and a pattern that seems to cover the world.

It has no better example than the religious scene in America. In many Christian churches a person of a different race would feel very unwelcome. The Pharisees were no better or worse at resolving this sickness.

In all fairness to the Pharisees, the Samaritans added considerably to the agitation by pestering the Jews. It is assumed that they are the "enemies" described in Ezra 4:2 who demanded their place in building the second temple and then tried to prevent it from being built.[4]

As time went on, the Samaritans developed quite dissimilar methods of worship, and the hate hung on. The Samaritans accepted only the first five books of the scriptures and built their own temple on Mount Gerizim.

When Jesus began his ministry, the hostility between the two groups was as blazing hot as it had been five centuries before. Josephus claims that the Samaritans had some access to the temple at Jerusalem, but around A.D. 6 to 9 they reportedly scattered human bones on the temple porches and all over the sanctuary during the night. This terrible desecration interrupted the Passover and raised the rage to new heights.

Into this raging storm walked the Son of God. He had a spiritual ministry, and it would have been tempting to advise him to steer clear of this squabble. After all, it was a temporal concern, the ministry was a higher calling, racial strife will always be with us. Nevertheless, it would appear that Jesus Christ did not make such a sharp distinction between the mundane and the mystical. Indeed, there is solid evidence that more than once he went out of his way to confront this very issue.

When Christ stopped to visit with the woman at the well in John chapter four, he was fully aware of the risk he was taking. By this time the "Jews do not associate with Samaritans" (John 4:9). Josephus tells us that Jewish guerillas would stage raids into Samaria and attack villages. The Samaritans reportedly murdered Galilean pilgrims going to a feast in Jerusalem.

The Jews consequently looked upon the Samaritans the

4. Bruce, *New International Commentary on the New Testament*, p. 104.

same way they regarded Gentiles. They openly cursed them in their synagogues, and their testimony was not allowed in a Jewish court. Even if a Samaritan decided he wanted to become a Jew, he would be refused and could not possibly inherit eternal life.[5]

Once we comprehend this deep-seated gut feeling between the two, we can understand some of the strange things that are recorded in the New Testament. For instance, Jesus and the Pharisees were having a very keyed-up discussion, and thoroughly angered, the Pharisees called Christ a dirty name. "Aren't we right in saying that you are a Samaritan and demon possessed?" (John 8:48). The Pharisees were not kidding themselves; they knew he was a Galilean and they thought him to be the son of Joseph. They were merely looking, out of frustration, for the nastiest thing they could call him, and it wasn't "nigger," "pollack," or "honky." It was "Samaritan," for there was no race they despised more.

This bit of background also helps us interpret a phrase in John 4:4, "Now he had to go through Samaria." It was further to go from Galilee, curve around Samaria, and head south for Judea. It would take approximately three days if you crossed Samaria and possibly twice as long if you went around, but people were choosing the longer route to avoid trouble.[6] Maybe there were numerous reasons why Christ "had to go" that way. To reach an individual, to share with a woman, and to give the Gospel to a hated Samaritan.

On another trip through Samaria Jesus met this exact opposition. He was going to travel to Jerusalem and sent messengers ahead of him. In one Samaritan village they wanted nothing to do with him because he was headed for Jerusalem. His disciples asked him to dump a little fire from heaven on the village just to teach them a lesson, but Jesus

5. Jeremias, op. cit., p. 354.
6. Robertson, op. cit., vol. 5, p. 60.

54

upbraided his disciples for such a low suggestion (Luke 9:51–56).

The air was thick with tension, and Jesus had the opportunity to skirt the issue and get on with the more "important issues." Jesus said no thanks—he had to go to the heart of where people lived. Large numbers of Christ's followers may have lost the vision and are reluctant to trace his example. For years many of us have argued that race and hate are not our problem, the church should avoid controversies. One must ask if Christ would have sat still in that box.

In the late 1960s I was invited to speak at a church in Michigan for a week of "evangelistic" meetings. I had been there a number of times before and had had good vibes with the congregation. Each year hundreds of migrant workers invaded the area to help pick fruit and vegetables. Toward the last night of the meetings I mentioned the fact that if I was the pastor of the church, I would go after the migrant workers.

A pastor almost gets used to silent stares after a service, but that day the stares were vocal. Some people were thoroughly insulted. The very thought of having such people in their sanctuary was repulsive, and they wanted me to know it. I asked one of the more vocal ones whether she would care to evangelize the Negro at all, and she replied, "Well, I certainly wouldn't go out of my way to do it."

Many churches have been lulled into this posture by believing that this was not part of Christ's ministry. His association with the Samaritans, to the dismay of the Pharisees, makes this position difficult to defend.

If we didn't know Christ better, we would be tempted to accuse him of going out of his way to shock people. Consider the familiar story of the ten lepers whom Jesus heals. Only one of the ten came back to thank Jesus, and the narrative curtly adds, "and he was a Samaritan" (Luke 17:11–19). Is it unfair to wonder why this is added? It didn't make the story more acceptable to the Pharisees, since they saw fire when they heard the word. Did Luke or Christ add that little description just to drive a point home? Was it a diplomatic blunder or an important plank in his ministry?

There is another story that Christ told and that may rank as one of the most familiar stories in the English language. It is the story of the Good Samaritan. One wonders why it wasn't the Good Pharisee, the Good Sadducee, or the Good Scribe. One must conclude that Jesus is calculating in what he says, and he is prepared to let the steam rise. In the story Christ makes a priest and a Levite both look selfish and afraid and the Samaritan look like Captain Marvel (Luke 10:25-37).

It would be like telling a Protestant group how well the Catholic served God, or telling a white congregation how the Caucasians chickened out and a "nigger" stopped by the side of the road and helped a man. That is exactly what the Pharisees heard when this story violated their minds.

Today we know the tale so well that we have overlearned it. We can hear it without really hearing it. In 1974 *Human Behavior* magazine conducted a test in a tricky manner. They asked a number of seminary students to prepare a short devotional on the Good Samaritan and report to a building to deliver it on the radio. The magazine staff then placed an actor to pretend he was sick on the path to the building. More than half of the students walked past him or even stepped over him because they were too busy preparing their message on the Good Samaritan.

One Christian asked his pastor to not speak on the subject of the Good Samaritan. He explained that the question of social concern was so touchy among the people that it would only cause trouble.

Pharisaism is not dead. It is a spirit that still fills the hearts of men of all stripes. It is at its worst when Christian Pharisees attempt to silence the words of Christ because he would interrupt our bigotry and call us to compassion for those who are different.

Questions for Further Thought

1. How did Matthew's job affect his life and attitudes?
2. Explain the attitudes of the Pharisees toward the tax collectors.
3. What unique features did Christ add in his attitude toward publicans?
4. Describe some outcast groups in our society and make some suggestions on how Christians can minister to them.
5. Why do you think Jesus needed to go through Samaria in John, chapter four?
6. Are Christ's actions toward the Samaritans relevant to our present society, or should we behave differently than he did?
7. Are there people in your local community who suffer from your religious, racial, or national bigotry?

6

A Special Piety

Paul Little told an audience at Urbana, Illinois, that meditation was the lost art of the West. Part of the attraction of
Eastern religions and cults is the fact that they call me away
from the complicated maze back to simple communication
with God.

A young lady planted a hoax on her dinner guests by serving salt in their summer drink. One of her visitors blurted
out jokingly, "How could anyone mess up iced tea?" It would
seem just as difficult to "mess up" something as basic as talking with God, but the Pharisees and their descendents
managed to foul it up.

Jesus said several things about the religions of his day that
should make us, as current Christians, scratch our heads.
None was more befuddling or harsher than what he told
them about widows and prayer. It would be easy to see it as
only a criticism of their handling of widows. But that would
be like calling the fire department to put out your smoke.

Before a large crowd he said, concerning the teachers of
the law, "They devour widows' houses and for a show make
lengthy prayers. Such men will be punished most severely"
(Luke 20:47 and Mark 12:40 and Matt. 23:14 in some ver-
sions).

We cannot say with precision exactly what was happening, but several options are open. A con game was being perpetrated at some level, and widows were being bilked out of their security. It may have been that the Pharisees were asking for more contributions from the widows than they really needed to give. It may be that they were charging for their teaching (a practice strictly forbidden). Or else they were in a bold-faced scheme to swindle widows out of their goods.

Whatever the case, Jesus understood and was all the more shocked because of their righteous position. People have always been outraged by this type of behavior, and yet it always persists. Christ was all the more dismayed because he was aware of the special care God had promised the widow, and to now watch "God's servants" violate their trust was all the more hideous to the Son of God.

The widow in ancient times faced an even harder road than she does today in Western societies. In fact the Hebrew word for *widow* is similar to the word meaning "be mute." This may have suggested the fact that she had been neutralized. She was without standing or voice in the community. If people did not step in to protect her interest, it became easy to take advantage of her. She even at times wore special garments so she could be readily identified (Gen. 38:14,19).

With this status in mind God laid out certain safeguards. He promised to provide her with food and clothing (Deut. 10:18) and he thunderously and repeatedly condemned anyone who dared play an injustice upon her (Isa. 11:23; 10:2; Ps. 94:6; etc.).

While pretending to uphold these very laws, the Pharisees cunningly relieved the widows of their money. Reports of this type of pious plundering are multiplied in ancient literature just as they could be documented today. The Pharisaic writer of the "Assumption of Moses" speaks out in hostility against people in his own order for doing this and condemns them for lacking mercy. The Midrash records the story of a woman who protests because the priests have made such large financial demands and her resources are so slender.

As Abrahams points out very well, moralists of all ages can well repeat the same complaint that Jesus uttered, and he admits that the Nazarene had ample room for such a denunciation, quoting the old rabbinic saying, "He who robs the widow and orphan is as though he robbed God himself." [1]

Are there no parallels in the twentieth century? Have not the churches asked, "What can the widows do for the church?" instead of "What can the church do for the widows?" Have we not often taken and taken and taken and given nothing in return? Have we not been the long multiple arms of an octopus when we collect and the cuffed hands when the same people are hungry?

Would it be indelicate to challenge the "stewardship" representatives, who may outdo themselves by encouraging an elderly person to "retithe" his income when he makes out his will? Do our concern for buildings and monuments outweigh our compassion for the widow left behind?

And far beyond the shoddy collectors, what about those who are overt frauds, those organizations that misrepresent their work, their goals, and their needs while they fleece the unsuspecting? The organization has learned to play on a tender heart, and the widow is moved compassionately for the "Lord's work."

A missions society in Maryland was investigated by the federal government because of its collection practices. They had spent a considerable sum for direct-mail solicitations, and they collected $15 million. However, their books indicated that they had sent $250,000 to the mission field. That is a lot of overhead for paper clips and stamps.

1. Abrahams, op. cit., p. 81.

Would it be unfair to ask if Christ would raise serious doubts about some of the causes that are espoused over "Christian radio"? Would he listen with sympathetic ears to that massive array of financial pleas? A strange assortment of plans and embellished programs, developed at the speaker's whim, and supported by the unwise listener. Would Christ remain silent at such contrived piety? All we know for certain is that he did not then.

As he often did, Jesus introduced a living visual aid to seal his lesson. He looked up at the temple treasury and saw a widow putting in two small copper coins, and he commended her action (Luke 21:1–4). This short story puts his complaint into perspective. Christ is not upset because widows give and they can't afford it. Sacrificial giving has always been a virtue and should be accepted in a correct spirit. However, that giving must be voluntarily inaugurated and not coerced.

Granted, there are many pressures squeezing the modern Christian organization, and its task is a burden. Nevertheless, we cannot allow such arguments of expediency to affect our judgment and lead us to unscrupulous, neo-Pharisaic practices.

Christ adds, in essence, "And just think, these pious plunderers parade with protracted prayers." He makes a decided distinction between shysters selling sugar water for cough medicine and ministers padding the church coffers. He teaches us that the latter are far worse and will receive the more severe punishment.

It is consistent with Christ's entire teachings that he offers more compassion for the man in the bar who knows he needs help than the self-righteous pew rider who thinks he is in excellent shape.

What religious experience is more hollow than a perfunctory prayer? Have you ever had someone discuss a problem with you and then pray because he seemingly knows no other way to end the conversation? He has failed to convey compassion or understanding or even interest, but now he knows that the "proper" thing to do is to close in prayer. What an atrocious abuse of a moment as precious as love itself. Sometimes our mind screams out at him, "Don't pray! You don't mean a word of it."

Christ charges these Pharisees with scraping a scab until it stings and bleeds and is covered with flies. There is no healing or comfort from someone who is out to get your money, and all the pretense only makes it uglier.

This practice did not merely violate Christ's conscience, it also was an affront to all sincere Jews. For him the heart of prayer was earnestness and feeling. Yet some had come far from that sacredness.

The Hebrew word for prayer may have as its origin a root that means "cuttings of the flesh." It points to the fact that when the Jew thought of prayer, he often pictured a man wrestling with God. Initially he didn't imagine a dispassionate, cleverly worded discourse on theology. The Jew did not pray a book review of the Old Testament, as the lead character in *Fiddler on the Roof* comically did. He tried to pour out his heart in joy, repentance, or desperation.

Abrahams tells us of an Essene named Onias, "the circle-drawer." He would tell people to cover their perishable goods because he was going to pray for rain. Then he would draw a circle around the place where he stood. Then he would start to plead with God and vow to not leave that circle until God did something about it.[2]

Many Jewish writers, both during the time of Christ and since, have been careful to protest the pretentious and haughty prayer. They hated to see prayer come off the assembly line like so many well-computerized sedans. Individual prayer was at the center of their religious experience, and its mesmerizing could only result in a monstrosity.

2. Ibid., pt. 2, pp. 73–74.

The Rabbis said, "Make not thy prayer a fixed thing but a supplication for mercy."

Despite these well-advised warnings prayer soon became more regimented than a marine-corps drill team. Soon certain times were set for prayer, then particular phrases were recommended to be repeated. Then whole prayers were selected for stated occasions. Others measured their prayer by the pound, like cheap bologna, rather than by its sincerity.

Unger tells us that saying grace at meals became a routine of stifling rigidness.[3] They developed certain prayers for fruit that came from a tree, another prayer for fruit from the ground, for breads, for vegetables, for milk, etc. It must have been invigorating to attend a board meeting to discuss which prayer would be suitable for fruitcake.

It is easy to see why many young Jews may have become frustrated at such strangling legalism. Life is filled with enough absurdities without manufacturing religious games.

In his Sermon on the Mount, Christ zeroed in on two specific perversions. First, they prayed for the purpose of being seen by others. Second, they prayed in endless rows of monotonous clichés.

"And when you pray, do not keep on babbling like pagans, for they think they will be heard because of their many words" (Matt. 6:7).

The implications of what Christ said may be more than many of us can bear. While we have repeatedly scorned the Pharisees, maybe we owe them an apology. We may have easily outdone them on both counts of Christ's indictment.

Some years ago I wrote an article for a magazine elaborating on the values of public prayer as a "testimony." In the light of Christ's words one has to wonder at the wisdom of wearing "I Am Righteous" buttons. Maybe saying

3. Merrill F. Unger, *Unger's Bible Dictionary* (Chicago: Moody Press, 1960), p. 430.

grace in a restaurant needs to be more a question of personal gratitude rather than a showcase for Christianity or a pressure to please other Christians.

The concept of an Oriental prayer wheel strikes most of us as ludicrous, but we may have outdone it. Our vain repetitions because it is time to pray again may be just as obnoxious to God as anything the old Pharisees had to offer.

In one Christian college the regular routine was to have a professor call on students to lead in prayer before each class. For many years names were rattled off in alphabetical order, and like Pavlov's dog, someone would pray. One day an instructor threw out a name, and everyone bowed their head like mechanical monkeys. Everyone sat silently waiting for the daily ritual. Soon eyes started to open and look around the room. Then a voice ended the suspense, "Professor, my heart isn't right to pray this morning."

When one ponders how many of us have so often reeled off a few thoughtless sentences, one may well be astonished that only one person ever said, "No thanks." Prayer meant too much to him to merely stack three sentences on a conveyor belt and pass them on.

Whatever else could be said about prayer at its best, it is heartfelt and voluntary. In the New Testament (as well as in the Old Testament) prayer has enormous flexibility. There are examples of very short prayer (Matt. 6:9–15), of long, intense prayer (Luke 6:12), of public (Luke 3:21) and private prayer (Mark 6:46). There are prayers of anguish (Luke 22:44) and prayers of joy (Acts 16:25) and continuous talking with God (1 Thess. 5:17).

Not only was prayer offered in every conceivable mood but also in a kaleidoscope of styles. Some prayed standing, others lay flat on the ground, still others bowed their heads between their legs. Many prayed with their hands raised in the air (1 Tim. 2:8), sometimes they cried, tore at their clothes, or beat on their chests like Tarzan in the jungle.

With this rich, vivacious mosaic description of prayer it is easy to see why both Jesus and many of his contempories hated to watch it become mummified. Prayer is not merely a luxury to be enjoyed by the highly disciplined. It is not a right reserved for only the punctual and diligent. Rather it is an open highway with a ready access for anyone, anytime, who cares to drive it.

Many of us lack the qualities of the stereotyped saint. Consequently we feel worthless because of our lack of persistence in effective prayer. Have heart! God is at least as interested in the man who dabbles at prayer as he is in the person who thinks he has mastered it. Hallesby's words should serve as a great boost for many of us:

"Thus an honest soul struggles against the dishonesty of his own being. He feels himself so helplessly lost that his prayers freeze on his lips.

"Listen, my friend! Your helplessness is your best prayer. It calls from your heart to the heart of God with greater effect than all your uttered pleas. He hears it from the very moment that you are seized with helplessness, and he becomes actively engaged at once in hearing and answering the prayer of your helplessness. He hears today as He heard the helpless and wordless prayer of the man sick with the palsy."[4]

With their aura of special piety the Pharisees were also able to play a similar game when it came to miracles. As with many other moral gymnasts, they believed in miracles without believing in miracles. Despite the obvious contradiction of the position, they managed to maintain their absurdity as have their neo-Pharisee descendants.

The Pharisees believed in the supernatural to a greater extent than did their antagonistic friends, the Sadducees. The Old Testament contained the theology of miracles, and Judaism generally took the concept for granted. Jeremiah

4. O. Hallesby, *Prayer* (Minneapolis: Augsburg Publishing House, 1936), p. 17.

spoke for many when he discerned, "Lord, you alone can heal me, you alone can save, and my praises are for you alone" (Jer. 17:14).

However, while they acknowledged the fact mentally, they were embarrassed to see any evidence of it. It had to be done quietly, even undiscernably, or else they were quick to deny it. Consequently they could say, "God heals men of leprosy." Excellent. A superb affirmation of faith in God's ability. But do not say, "God healed Mr. Brown of leprosy." Immediately the Pharisees became suspicious to hostile. The minute a miracle became close or concrete, they stroked their beards instead of jumping up and down.

Consider a case in point when Jesus healed a man who had been blind since his birth (John 9). Three options were open to the Pharisees at this stage. They could accept the fact that Jesus had performed a documented miracle. They could take a noncommittal position and investigate the event. They could summarily denounce the miracle as a fraud and then attempt to prove the assumed hoax. Without batting an eye, they took the third position.

This learned reflex says more about the Pharisees than the story itself. They had developed an *a priori* negative outlook on God, religion, and all of life. They had become inbred skeptics. They blatantly considered anything that they did not understand as threatening and dangerous.

At a twentieth-century "ministers' retreat" a bright, articulate seminary professor was asked if he thought Dave Wilkerson really had a special "vision" from God. What a refreshing change to hear him say, "I really don't know, but I would not want to restrict what God might do." It was a far cry from the distrustful spirit that automatically labels every supernatural display as sheer imitation.

The Pharisees' feeble attempts couldn't deny the fact that something happened to the gentleman in question. Great crowds had seen the blind beggars near the pool of Siloam for years. They became defensive immediately, and their objections popped up like corks under pressure. Jesus did it on the wrong day. Jesus was a sinner. Like children caught with cookies in their hands, they sputtered to make excuses.

In their special piety they knew that God would not perform such a spectacular miracle. They also knew that God would not work through such a lowlife as Jesus. After all, they had made special laws to prevent people from believing in him and threatened expulsion from the synagogue for anyone who claimed he was the Messiah (John 9:22).

Their logic was as simple as it was blasphemous. If God was working in this man, the Pharisees would say so. Since they, with their piety, rejected the evidence, it was plain that he was an imposter. They did not imply that they were the final judges of what was righteous, they boldly said so. They explained to the temple guards why Jesus was not the Christ.

"You mean he deceived you also?" the Pharisees retorted. "Have any of the rulers of the Pharisees put their trust in him? No! But this mob that knows nothing of the law—there is a curse on them" (John 7:47–49).

Distrustful of God's measuring rod for piety, they thought they had better make sure and develop their own. Their self-righteous brothers followed them immediately after the church was founded. Paul had to rattle their cage by exposing their *modus operandi*.

"When they measure themselves by themselves and compare themselves with themselves, they are not wise" (2 Cor. 10:12).

In the past God spoke to many people through dreams. Can we be so sure that he does not today? It may be dangerous to encourage people to sift out dreams, but it is equally hazardous to edict that God cannot speak that way.

It is easy to be suspicious of people who claim that God

"spoke" to them. Yet the Bible, history, and current experience are all replete with accounts of "traditional" Christians who benefited from such an encounter.

Coming from a noncharismatic orientation, I personally find it fascinating to watch the double-jointed contortions that people do to try to disprove certain gifts. Almost as though the year A.D. 70 and the destruction of the temple made a giant eraser to eradicate the problems we cannot otherwise handle.

It is one thing to deny charlatan claims. It is quite another to reject behavior that has clear Biblical precedence and instruction. It takes a "special piety" to try that.

When Jesus laid out his credentials, they were carefully documented in the Old Testament. John specifically asked to see the proof, and Christ was glad to produce it.

He told John's disciples, "Go back and report to John what you hear and see. The blind receive sight, the lame walk, those who have leprosy are cured, the deaf hear, the dead are raised, and the good news is preached to the poor" (Matt. 11:4,5). In saying that, he quoted from Isa. 35:5,6 and Isa. 61:1.

Unfortunately the Pharisees were no longer the humble interpreters of the law. Now they had become rulers of piety and they decided to put their own peculiar straitjacket on God.

Questions for Further Thought

1. What did Jesus mean when he said Pharisees had "devoured widows' houses"?
2. Are there any present-day parellels?
3. Why was Christ insulted by their long prayers?
4. What was Christ's twofold complaint before he gave the "Lord's Prayer"?

5. Why do you think people pray so little?
6. Why did Jesus heal the blind man in John chapter nine?
7. Why did the Pharisees object to this miracle?

7
Playing with the Law

A college dean felt that his school was running under the honor system. The faculty had the honor, and the students had the system. Many aspects of a religious life are conducted on the same basis: God has the honor and the worshipers have the system.

The Pharisees had reduced the game of "evasive morality" to a fine art. They set the pace for the modern employer who underpays employees on Friday and sings hymns on Sunday and for the realtor who sells swampland on Monday and serves on the church board on Tuesday. When truth becomes an option rather than a necessity, we all join the corps that Christ so amply referred to as blind fools and hypocrites.

Christ indicted the fraternity for the absurd practice of playing games to avoid keeping their promises. The description of the practice sounds more like two four-year-olds playing marbles than the actions of the religious leaders of Israel. When they made a promise, they would swear on the temple that they would keep it. But, alas, their word meant nothing if they did not swear by the gold of the temple (Matt. 23:16–22). They could likewise swear by the altar, but their word was worthless unless they swore by the gift on the altar.

This isn't a very flattering picture—grown men crossing their fingers and then laughing because they fooled someone—but this is exactly the case. Some respectable scholars feel the illustrations given by Christ are so burlesque that they cannot possibly be accurate. Barclay says that the description is more likely *reductio ad absurdum* than a literal fact.[1]

It is easy to appreciate the reluctance to accept the account at face value. Certainly Christ had the right to use a dramatic overstatement, and he probably did in the account of the blowing of trumpets as their gifts were given (Matt. 6:2). However, in this instance there is good historical precedence.

The Mishnah, dating to 150 years after Christ, refers to a similar childish perversion of the truth. It states (Shebu. 4:13) that if one adjures someone by heaven and earth, the promise is not binding. If, however, he swears by the divine names, it is binding.[2]

The exact meaning of the temple gold is not clear, and the reader may choose. There was gold laid around the temple itself, or else it refers to the temple treasury, which is called corban. There was certainly an ample supply of gold, as some historians tell us Crassus transplanted eight thousand talents of it when he sacked the temple.

The insanity of this situation would be unbelievable if we did not see it so often in our present world. The morality, the ethics, the fairness, the personal integrity are not even an issue among some religious leaders. The whole question is whether or not they have been able to skirt a promise that they knowingly made. From the very start they intended to deceive the person and made provisions to get away with it. (And they did not trust tax collectors or Samaritans to testify in their courts.)

1. William Barclay, *The Gospel of Matthew* (Philadelphia: The Westminister Press, 1958), p. 323.
2. Buttrick, op. cit., vol. 3, p. 577.

Was Jesus merely being picky about a system that everyone understood and went along with? Was Jesus splitting hairs when the important things of life were the large issues of God, heaven, and the atonement? It is amazing how many Christians consider personal ethics to be far down on the list of important factors in being a disciple of Christ.

Among some Christians there is almost a discernible pattern to sidestep personal responsibility. It is almost laughable to watch hundreds of people pack a church to have a speaker dazzle an audience with the latest fads in prophecy. Couples go home humming about the rebuilding of the temple. Will it be before the rapture or after? What do all of those horses in Arabia mean? Does the Pope have three sixes inside his cap?

People are obviously excited—excited about the detached and impersonal. They have succeeded in constructing a glass bubble around themselves to shield out the parts of the gospel that grapple with heart and conscience. Would a week of meetings on the Sermon on the Mount cause as much stir? Quite the contrary. Some of these same people are suspicious of that sermon and feel it is not for the present age. Consequently, many of the problems concerning race, low wages, and deception go unanswered because some conservatives do not consider them relevant to the Christian life.

Christ was terribly bothered by the callousness to personal ethics and very plainly told the Pharisees so. Would it not be safe to assume that he would do the same to us today?

No passage of scripture depicts this more clearly than what he told the Pharisees concerning their habits in tithing.

"You give a tenth of your spices—mint, dill and cumin. But you neglect the more important matters of the law . . . justice, mercy and faithfulness" (Matt. 23:23).

Tithing was very important under the Old Testament system, and Christ does not condemn them for the practice as such. It meant that faithful Jews were to give away 10 percent of their produce and earnings. These gifts were to be used to support the Levites, who helped maintain the worship facilities. The Levites in turn tithed those gifts to support the high priest. There was more than one tithe given by the average Jew, and the Bible outlines a complicated but thorough method of giving.

Precisely what is Christ's beef concerning the Pharisaic practice? Barclay feels that they were being too picky about tithing every little seed in their kitchen.[3] Though he is an excellent scholar, it is again necessary to disagree with him. The Old Testament emphatically states that seeds are to be tithed. Deut. 14:22 states, "You must tithe all of your crops every year." (King James has *seed*.)

It is also clear from the corresponding passage in Luke 11:42 that Christ is not rattled by the things they are tithing. Both passages add this sentence, "You should have practiced the latter without leaving the former undone." Jesus did not disapprove of the practice, whatever his intentions for the church may have been.

Both the Talmud and the Mishnah record some of the extreme attitudes held by some Jews. One rabbi reportedly even had a donkey who was so well trained that he would refuse to eat corn that had not been properly tithed. (Someone's imagination was working overtime.) Some rabbis felt that if a wife set untithed food before her husband, he had ample grounds for divorce. Rabbi Simeon, son of Gamaliel, felt that the little buds or sprays of fennel and mustard were subject to the tithe.

When we put these facts together, what is the picture that takes form? There is an Old Testament obligation to tithe, and Christ does not dispute that. However, while they were so meticulously counting seeds lest they cheat God, they in

3. Barclay, op. cit., pp. 324, 325.

fact were cheating both God and man. Justice, mercy, and faithfulness are matters that involve our treatment of our fellow man, and Jesus placed these in the first magnitude. Their very concept of a righteous life had become such a super-spiritual experience that it could exist completely void of compassion and feeling for others. No place is this better demonstrated than in the present disregard for the needs and feelings of our companions on earth.

Some Christians are actually proud of the fact that they are not interested in justice or mercy. To help people who are unjustly imprisoned would be considered by some as an act of treason against the gospel. The issue is not spiritual enough. They do not deal with heaven or hell or the temple during the tribulation. Others look with disdain on the necessity to feed the hungry unless it is used as a carrot for evangelism.

For too many it actually becomes a game of words. They imagine that God loves men without loving them. As if by letting men die, we have done them a favor. It is the same mentality that hates someone in feelings and actions, but denies such hate because the Bible tells him he cannot hate. Man plays this game so frequently that he comes to believe that God is engaged in the same foolishness.

Christ tells us, Don't sit back and count seeds and say, look, I am spiritual. James said, Show me your faith without your works and I will show you my faith by my works.

Dr. Carl F. Henry has placed this ancient dilemma into current perspective:

> For Fundamentalism in practice requires the believer to abstain from certain "social evils" in order to be acceptable with God—and with other Fundamentalists. Christian ethics thereby becomes an index of legalistic "don'ts." One who is truly born again, it is insisted, does not smoke, dance, go to the theater, gamble, drink.

Without question, genuine regeneration issues in a marked change in character. But this negativism in Fundamentalists' ethics may conceal the fact that one who abstains from the prescribed may be every bit as carnal as one who indulges. Arbitrary legalism is a poor substitute for an inner morality. Not only this, but such legalism emphasizes the less important issues in life, and ignores or excuses the weightier matters of the Law. Smoking can be a subject of legislation; pride cannot.[4]

If such a tight-fisted, unloving concept of faith did not originate with Christ, was it born in the Old Testament? For all of their precise rules, Moses and his friends will not allow this charge to be pinned on them. While it is true that they were sticklers for detail, the Mosaic law did not neglect the more important things in life.

Abundant mercy was guaranteed for the poor in Israel, and any God-fearing Jew was obligated to help. Deut. 15:7,8, "But, if, when you arrive in the land the Lord will give you, there are among you those who are poor, you must not shut your heart or hand against them; you must lend them as much as they need."

Any poor person had the right to enter a field if he was destitute (Deut. 23:24,25). Each Israelite had the right to pick grapes and eat corn, though he was not allowed to carry it off in containers.

Every three years they laid up special tithes to help the stranger, the fatherless, and the widow (Deut. 14:28,29). In turn God promised to bless the people.

During the Sabbatical year special provision was made for the needy (Exod. 23:11). The Israelite was forbidden to charge interest on a loan to the poor, nor could he loan him food for profit (Lev. 25:35,36). Farmers were forbidden to

4. Carl F. H. Henry, *Christian Personal Ethics* (Grand Rapids: Wm. B. Eerdmans Publishing Co., 1957), p. 421.

clean off their fields at harvest in order that the poor could help themselves, and the corners of the fields were to be left unpicked for the sake of the hungry and for travelers (Lev. 23:22).

The inbred, self-centered, ultraspiritual aspect of Judaism and Christianity are purely the inventions of man. Christ did not come to destroy the law. It was not dedicated to the picky and petty. He came to call us to the highest possible law. A law written into the hearts of men that raises them to involvement in others.

The Pharisees whom Christ met had another peculiar habit that allowed them to play havoc with God's laws. When their parents were in financial need, some from this "holy" order would simply reply, "Corban," and ignore their responsibility.

The word occurs only once in the New Testament, but it contains a wealth of information. Jesus was reminding the Pharisees of their responsibility to their parents.

"For Moses, said, 'Honor your father and mother,' and 'Anyone who curses his father or mother must be put to death.' But I say that if a man says to his father or mother: 'Whatever help you might otherwise have received from me is Corban' (that is, a gift devoted to God), then you no longer let him do anything for his father or mother" (Mark 7:10–12). Matthew 15:5 is basically the same text.

The term *corban* refers to any gift dedicated to God and appears in one form or another in seventy passages in the Old Testament. The New Testament word for the temple treasury is another form of this same word (Matt. 27:6). Consequently if someone has promised to give something to God, that gift has become "corban," whether it has actually been delivered or not.

Possibly the scene is best comprehended by this illustration. Suppose a farmer has designated a field to be sold after he dies and the proceeds to be given to the temple. However, while he is still healthy, his parents fall into financial disaster. Their son then replies that he can't use the field to help his parents because it is corban—a gift to God.

Christ says, Nonsense. God does not allow us to treat human beings this way. The laws of God were not written to hurt people but to help them. We should not contort those laws until they become a curse without heart or feelings.

Again, we must call for fairness. Doubtless not all of the Pharisees did this, but most assuredly some of those whom Christ met practiced this very absurdity. There is abundant historical evidence that points to this aberrance.

The Mishnah states that anything that had been set aside by the use of the word, even if just for a while, and even if it was done rashly, could not be used for any other purpose. Vine claims the rabbis accepted and defended this practice and would say, "It is hard for the parents, but the law is clear, vows must be kept."[5]

For those who wanted to press the issue of keeping the vows there is plenty of evidence, of which Eccles. 5:4,5 is only a part. But Christ was not committed to a brittle, mindless interpretation of the scriptures. As he told the Pharisees on another occasion, the Sabbath was made for man and not man made for the Sabbath. The laws of God were constructed to help and not to hinder. God instructed us to both give to the temple and also take care of our parents, and not to use one as an excuse to avoid the other.

The theme sounded by Christ in the Gospels is reiterated in the early days of the church. Paul taught us to provide for our widows and other members of our family. They are our responsibility before they become wards of the state or the church. "If anyone does not provide for his relatives, and especially for his immediate family, he has denied the faith and is worse than an unbeliever." (1 Tim. 5:8)

5. W. E. Vine, *An Expository Dictionary of New Testament Words* (London: Oliphants Ltd., 1959), p. 240.

What we have been discussing in this chapter has dealt with some of the symptoms. Mickey Mousing around with oaths, taking painful particulars with tithing, and using the scriptures to dodge their duties are only surface sores. Inside there was a more basic philosophical and theological illness. These were only the fever, but Christ went further and identified the infection.

Repeatedly Jesus gives the same diagnosis:

"You have let go of the commandments of God and are holding on to the traditions of men" (Mark 7:8).

"Thus you nullify the word of God by your tradition that you have handed down. And you do many things like that"' (Mark 7:13; Matt. 15).

The traditions of the elders had become very numerous and were becoming more sophisticated. We have referred often to the Mishnah (or Mishna). The Jews had two sets of laws: those that were written in the Scriptures and those that were handed down orally. Rabbi Judah the Prince (born A.D. 135) compiled these oral or traditional laws into a codified written form. It included all of the currently accepted Jewish religious and legal systems of his day.

Most of the contributing rabbis were Pharisees.[6] They felt the need for changing laws since they thought that new experiences necessitated it. The Mishnah is divided into six divisions and includes 523 chapters. It probably was never intended to be accepted as absolute law but only as a lasting collection of sage sayings. These laws were well in vogue during the time of Christ even if they were not written down until the second century (Abrahams notwithstanding).

Again, in order to be fair we must be careful to determine just what Christ has said. He is not objecting to the traditions. Tradition can be both healthy and uplifting. What has upset Jesus runs in two directions. First, they make their

6. Nathan Ausubel, *The Book of Jewish Knowledge* (New York: Crown Publishers, Inc., 1947), pp. 442ff.

traditions as important as the scriptures. Second, they insist that everyone else keep their traditions. In short, they are monkeying with the commandments of God, and Christ refuses to permit it.

This is the reason why some observers call the Pharisees the liberals of Judaism. They felt very adjustable and were not reluctant to add whatever laws they felt were helpful. Likewise they were not afraid of dropping off a few laws if they found it preferable.

It is just as fruitless to try to label people as strict liberals or conservatives today. Some believers to the right of Christianity are prone to add entire lists of contemporary laws. Others who pride themselves in their liberalness nevertheless hold to some very basic biblical doctrines.

One day a pastor was explaining why a certain congregation did not appreciate his preaching. "I am just too Bible-centered for that group." I had heard him speak, and the minute he said this, I thought that he was the most non-biblical, mushy preacher I had ever heard. But that experience taught me that practically every Christian claims a devotion to the Bible. That is what makes it so difficult for each of us to admit that we are mixing a lot of our own personal laws into our faith and accepting them as divine.

Some churches have their own editions of the Mishnah, and others are intent on writing one. The more organized we become, the more some of us want extra laws to govern our conduct and personal morality. The logic starts off gentle enough. After all, we don't want anyone on the board who drinks wine, so we will write a law against it. We don't want anyone teaching Sunday school who plays cards—let's write a law against that.

It is not long until those laws, which began as opinions, move smoothly to commandments, then become even greater than the injunctions in the Bible itself. Sound preposterous? A pastor said he had tried hard to teach the scriptures as honestly and as boldly as he could. People scratched their heads, were puzzled at his conclusions, and doubted his orthodoxy. But as he said, "If I had spoken out against long hair or short skirts, everyone would have remarked how sound and fundamental I was."

In some segments of modern Christianity the "great truths" have boiled down to this. We are trying to read our life-style into the Bible rather than find guidance from it.

Every time I hear of another denomination or local church that is planning to make up a list of pet rules, my heart shrinks. How—but how—does this differ from what Christ clearly condemned? Has the Bible failed so badly that it cannot be our final authority for faith and practice? Has God been waiting all these years for us to put the crowning glory on truth by adding our traditions to the gallery of eternal laws? Such arrogance!

The Pharisaic attitude leaped rapidly into the very beginning of the church. Paul, who was delivered from that foul practice, wrote to the church at Colossae and gave them a happy encouragement:

"See to it that no one takes you captive through hollow and deceptive philosophy, which depends on human tradition and the basic principles of this world rather than on Christ" (Col. 2:8).

For those who played with God's laws during the time of Christ and those who play with them today his words still apply. By adding our laws we "nullify" the word of God—we don't help it.

Questions for Further Thought

1. What was the Pharisees' practice concerning making oaths?

2. In your opinion, are Christians more honest than non-Christians? Or vice versa?

3. If you are going to buy a used car, would you look for a Christian salesman? Why?

4. What do you feel was Christ's opinion of tithing? What is yours?

5. Explain why the Pharisees exclaimed, "Corban."

6. How important were the oral traditions to the Pharisees?

7. Can you think of some local Christian traditions that are as strong as the Bible itself?

8
Experienced Evangelists

When we think of evangelism, it is easy to conjure up visions of Jonathan Edwards standing by the crest of a hill in Massachusetts or see Billy Graham captivating 100,000 people at the Rose Bowl. However, these are only very limited views of a practice that has been carried on by different religions, in varying styles, for many centuries.

In the same way that the United States has seen several revivals mushroom across the country, so the Jews have experienced notable success in evangelism. Probably the most effective and widespread influx of converts came during the time of Christ. Under the heavy influence of the Pharisees Judaism had three hundred years of aggressive and effective evangelism.

The casual reader of the New Testament has often been bewildered by Christ's reference to the incorporation of Jewish converts.

"Woe to you, teachers of the law and Pharisees, you hypocrites! You travel over land and sea to win a single convert, and when he becomes one, you make him twice as much a son of hell as you are" (Matthew 23:15).

There is no way to soften these words. Christ is speaking

of a group who are very sincere for their religion, even to the point of being militant. They are so convinced concerning the merits of Judaism that they are willing to recommend it to others. These attitudes represent zeal, commitment, and strength. Nevertheless, Jesus, a fellow Jew, tells them that their proselytes are not only no better off but they are now "twice the sons of hell."

With our eellike agility most of us are persuaded that if Christ could talk to us, he would never pour such acid on our efforts at evangelism. After all, we do have a peculiar place with God. The Pharisees felt exactly the same way for precisely the same reasons. A close look might prove helpful to every branch of Christianity that is dedicated to making conversions.

During the "Golden Age" that we referred to earlier the Pharisees were riding a high crest of popularity and productivity. Judaism taught that an individual could experience a spiritual conversion and referred to it as the "new creation" or "new birth" in exactly the same fashion as Christ (John 3:3) and Paul (2 Cor. 5:17) did. When a proselyte was welcomed into the Jewish faith, it was said of him that he was now "under the wings of the Divine Presence." This is the same designation that had been given by Boaz to Ruth (2:12).

Since conversion was both possible and necessary, Jews throughout the world made attempts at evangelism. Part of the appeal that Judaism had was its monotheism in the light of repulsive paganism in the Roman Empire. Many Greeks were becoming tired of worshiping many, and sometimes contradictory, gods. Others were disillusioned with the guidance offered by the spectrum of philosophers. Still another segment found the moral values of the Jews to be more appealing.

Into this growing vacuum the Jews moved very aggressively. Despite their placid image they became extremely flexible and accommodated their style to appeal to the Greeks. A Gentile could hear some synagogue services in Greek, and special literature was written especially for foreigners. The wisdom of Solomon was compiled during this period for the purpose of blending Hellenistic and Judaistic propaganda. Aristobulus added his pen to try to reconcile the two ideologies. While we do not suggest that the Jews changed any laws to please the Greeks, they may well have chosen to expediently ignore a few.[1]

Whatever means they employed and whatever adjustments they may have conceded, they were very successful at evangelism. Some of their writers bragged of their accomplishments in this regard.[2] They won converts in practically every part of the world, and every city of any size had a Jewish community. No better compliment could be paid to their progress than the amount of opposition they received. The Roman government charged them with trying to infect their citizens with the Jewish religion and had the chief propagandist expelled as early as 139 B.C. Their zeal also accounts for the Jewish-Gentiles who are mentioned in the New Testament accounts.

There were three basic requirements for a proselyte after he took instruction from a scribe. Converts needed to be circumcised, baptized, and offer a sacrifice. There was a lot of debate over these rites, and consequently not everyone performed all three.

Circumcision involved painful surgery, and this probably explains why women converts greatly outnumbered the males. It also tells us why so many proselytes were described as "God-fearing" (for example, Cornelius, Acts 10:2). They

1. Buttrick, *op. cit.*, vol. 3, pp. 921ff.
2. Josephus, *Wars*, trans. William Whiston (Grand Rapids: Kregel Publications, 1969), II XX2.

held to the precepts of Judaism but they had stopped short of full initiation.

To this point Christ certainly had no major objections to the outline of their activity. However, evangelism is one problem; the question of what one does with the convert is entirely another. In our day it is one thing to invite someone to become a follower of Christ and it is quite another to instruct him afterward. It is not uncommon for someone to believe in or accept Christ and then have some individual lay all sorts of laws on him that would be strange to Christ and the New Testament.

When someone became a Jew by adoption, legally he had the same right to acceptance as anyone who was born to Judaism. Often these were only promises that never matured into facts. The Hillel branch of the Pharisees were very liberal and open to proselytes. Their attitude was, "Let's get them in and make them part of us." Those from the Shammai branch were a little more cautious. They were suspicious of foreigners and were all for testing the newcomer's motives and going slowly. Some were very blunt and considered these converts a leprosy in Israel.

This is the place where Jesus became outraged. The Pharisees wanted to take legitimate converts and turn the "converted into the perverted." They wanted to pile myriads of cheap, little laws on innocent, eager new believers, and Christ was beside himself. When they were finished with them, their love for God would be shredded until nothing remained but a list of infantile regulations.

It is the same charge he leveled at them in the beginning of the chapter. "They tie up heavy loads and put them on men's shoulders, but they themselves are not willing to lift a finger to stop them" (Matt. 23:4).

There was a distinct feeling that placing extra moral loads on converts was not only necessary but was very helpful. As some people today are fond of saying, "Well, the church has to have some sort of standard." The motto sounds plausible enough. But does this mean that Christians need *any* standard no matter how arbitrary it is? Why not make it immoral to skip rope or declare boating as godless?

For all the debates over moral and practical behavior, the real basic issue goes back to the question of authority. Is the Scripture the final word, or do we have a right to add our fickle mores as though they had divine origin? Some of the Pharisees felt that additional data was necessary to update their practical theology.

Before we jeer the old fraternity, we might well turn our antennae inward. How many times have we supported "extra-Biblical" prerequisites to church membership and insisted that we were protecting God's assembly?

Shammai had written, "Make thy Torah a fixed thing; so that thou are neither easier or harder to thyself then to others." This approach sounds noble; however, in fact it meant that laws could be added, but once accumulated, were almost never deleted.

This was a major part of Christ's complaint. They were great at adding new laws and terrible at removing old ones. Consequently the laws piled high until they became so cumbersome that they staggered the dedicated novice. Israel Abrahams objects at this point and correctly insists that there were rabbis who removed obsolete commandments.[3] The Pharisaic leader Hillel was probably as good as anyone at offering relief. This point is well taken; however, Abrahams also admits that Hillel's group of Pharisees were most likely in the minority during the life of Christ. Many Pharisees (and thousands of other religious leaders) were completely inflexible in this regard.

Their rigidness contributed heavily to the popularity of

3. Abrahams, op cit., pt. 2, pp. 10–12.

Jesus Christ. Then, as now, many people were getting fed up with the rigors of a religious straitjacket. Consequently, when we couple the facts of Matt. 23:4 with what Christ said in Matt. 11:28–30, we see the sharp contrast:

"Come unto me, all you who are weary and burdened, and I will give you rest. Take my yoke upon you and learn from me, for I am gentle and humble in heart, and you will find rest for your souls. For my yoke is easy and my burden is light."

For many Christians this passage has been perplexing. After all, Christ did talk about the hardships of following him (for instance, putting one's hand to the plow, hating mother and father, letting the dead bury the dead, they will curse us and think they have done God a favor). None of that sounds easy or light.

However, we come closer to understanding Christ by comparing these words with the Pharisees. They offered an unbearable burden of picky rules in an effort to keep man quiet and God pacified. Jesus Christ offered a challenging, though dangerous, opportunity to serve God and to help men find him.

For Christ it was not difficult to find peace with God. He had carved out a yoke that was well-fitting and comfortable to carry. To his followers God was not a growling drill instructor with white gloves barking orders and humiliating us for our weaknesses. Nor was he an ancient despot who lopped off heads when he felt disgruntled.

Jesus talked about gentleness and humility. This was a clear contrast to certain Pharisees, who prided themselves in rigidness. They felt that arrogance and intolerance were their strength. Christ did not ask for a man's pettiness—he only asked for his life.

There can be no doubt that this was Christ's message and that it was very clear to his disciples. During the famous Council of Jerusalem this exact issue arose to confront the young church. Men who had previously been Pharisees had become believers in Christ. Since their background had been inundated with laws rather than grace, they still found the adjustment difficult. Consequently, they insisted that Gentile converts to Christianity had to be circumcised and keep the laws. This council was particularly crucial to Christianity. If the law lobby won, the church would become little more than neo-Pharisaism. The implications were shattering. At that point Christianity could have lost its uniqueness and degenerated into another branch of Judaism.

Fortunately, it was one of Peter's stronger moments, and he rose eloquently to the occasion:

"Now then, why do you try to test God by putting on the necks of the disciples a yoke that neither we nor our fathers have been able to bear? No! We believe it is through the grace of our Lord Jesus that we are saved, just as they are" (Acts 15:10,11).

The battle continued throughout the history of the church despite this clear stand. To Christianity's credit, it is committed to a stand of grace and the position of personal priesthood. This posture is well documented in both the New Testament and numerous reaffirmations since. To the church's discredit, it is sometimes enslaved to the very laws that it claims do not exist.

There are many churches that have no "extra" laws in written form, and they pride themselves in that fact. Nevertheless, their unwritten laws are stronger than any printed form could ever be. Everyone knows which practices and behavior are acceptable and which are not. The person who indiscreetly violates these codes finds himself a second-class parishioner. And this is exactly the way many members are convinced it should be. With God's laws on one side and our laws on the other we can keep anyone in check.

When Martin Luther reintroduced the doctrine of the

universal priesthood of believers, he sounded a daring note of independence for the Christian. This is the very sound that many consider to be dangerous today.

By the time Paul wrote to the churches of Galatia, the dastardly debate was raging hot again. How can a Christian be a Christian with a steady dose of the law? Even the stalwarts of grace such as Peter, the noted orator at Jerusalem, had reversed their field. Now they wanted proselytes to become Jews first and Christians afterward. Paul kept a cool head and realized the monumental issues at stake. He faced Peter down in front of everyone and called him into account. His accusation of hypocrite is thinly veiled.

"You are a Jew, yet you live like a Gentile and not like a Jew. How is it, then, that you force Gentiles to follow Jewish customs?" (Gal. 2:14b).

One can almost feel the terrible struggle that went on in Peter's heart. His background was also flooded with this conflict. He was reluctant to allow Gentiles to become Christians at first, but God convinced him otherwise and sent him to see Cornelius (Acts 10). Then he defended the full rights of Gentiles (Acts 15). Now he wonders if it won't be better if Gentiles became Christians via Judaism, and yet he enjoys the liberty of being freed from the law. What a mixed salad of conscience it is that qualifies him as the grandfather of most of us.

Paul, at least for the time being, seems to have it sifted out well and champions the cause of grace for converts:

"It is for freedom that Christ has set us free. Stand firm, then, and do not let yourselves be burdened again by a yoke of slavery" (Gal. 5:1).

Yet it is argued that the more strict groups with the extensive lists of moralistic demands are the churches that grow. This claim carries considerable truth to it. But are we so pragmatic as to suggest that if people respond to severe regimentation, we should use it? Isn't there a far more important question of whether it is right or wrong rather than an expedient wisp of "does it work"?

Surely many Christians are in fact the sons of Peter in this regard. We don't want new converts to become enslaved. Neither do we want them to fall into lawlessness. And yet the principles of living by grace are too revolutionary to find rest in our hearts. For many sincere Christians it presents a number of unsettling conflicts.

Be careful to understand. Neither Jesus nor Paul were advocating lawlessness. Rather they were defending personal moral responsibility before God. They were rejecting accountability to fellow Christians that necessitated keeping a man-made moral code.

In discussing a case, Dr. Paul Tournier explains the difference well:

"Faced with these two opposing views of the case at hand, it seemed to me that on Christian grounds it was possible to arrive at a perfectly clear conclusion: complete absence of legal responsibility, but complete personal moral responsibility." [4]

To this discussion Jesus added a puzzling but helpful phrase, "So you must obey them and do everything they tell you. But do not do what they do, for they do not practice what they preach" (Matt. 23:3).

This part of Christ's analysis has often been a bewilderment. After all, it has always been conceded, even by Jesus himself, that the Pharisees were nit-pickers concerning the law. However, it becomes apparent what he meant when he addressed them on subjects such as tithing. There he accused them of tithing every piece of lint and yet neglecting the more important parts of the law such as justice, mercy, and faithfulness (Matt. 23:23).

Comparing these two passages, we may conclude that the

4. Paul Tournier, *The Person Reborn* (New York: Harper and Row, Publishers, 1966), p. 116.

Pharisees had become armchair moralists.[5] They taught the entire law; both the Mosaic and their homespun editions. They outlined both the regulatory laws and the great moral issues. Yet, while teaching the precepts of forgiveness, love, and tolerance, they did not lift a finger to obey them.

These issues transcend the immediate problem of Pharisaism. It broaches the very nature of man. How many people were shocked at the vocabulary used by President Nixon, and yet they use the same words? How many people hate people who hate people? How many are upset at the overt sex they watch on television—that they watch on television.

The Pharisees had lost their humility as well as their tolerance. They set up hurdles that they did not intend to jump.

This does not imply that it is wrong to be against, for instance, overeating, if you overeat. It is perfectly logical for someone to be opposed to his own overeating. But what is reprehensible is to condemn my brother for overeating while I overeat.

The Pharisees failed in their obligation to the new converts by demanding a morality that they themselves did not keep. Is it any wonder that young believers would then develop a callousness to the guidance of God?

Morality must have humility. Otherwise we lose contact with our own frailty—indeed our own humanity. Once we believe that we are inherently different from the thief or the prostitute, we have lost touch with reality.

Jesus would have them teach the great theology of morality with arrogance. He would also have them lift a finger to keep it.

It would be hard to calculate how many young people, from nonchurched families, have become Christians only to discover terrible disillusionment. They discovered that those

5. Abrahams, op. cit., pt. 2, pp. 4–14.

who condemned gossip so ferociously were themselves gossips. Those who were so intolerant of stealing were not above cheating. Soon the convert's idealism settles into a similar hypocritical pattern.

Far better had he entered Christianity knowing that we are all a bunch of vagabonds in need of the grace of God. Far better to find mutual help rather than relentless judgment.

The phenomenal success that Jewish evangelism experienced for almost three hundred years ground to a halt and probably has never been equaled. Several circumstances met during the first century to stall the movement. The temple in Jerusalem was destroyed in A.D. 70, and Judaism lost its important focal point. While Judaism was not declared illegal, at least four Roman emperors forbade the conversion of Gentiles. A third reason may have been an increased feeling against and distrust of foreigners. There can be no doubt that the influx of Gentiles was making noticeable alterations in Judaism in some localities. Fourth may be the rise in Christianity. Despite the fact that Christianity was illegal, many died to join it, and persecution seemed to cause it to mushroom. Christianity may have become a preferable alternative to Judaism in spite of the danger.

Some rabbis encouraged each member of their congregation to win one convert per year. Christ also encouraged his followers to bring in the lost. However, he knew that young plants were easily bent by strong, relentless winds. He was concerned that perverted men would convert a man and make him worse off than he had ever been.

Questions for Further Thought

1. Why did Greeks turn to Judaism?
2. What were the requirements for conversion to Judaism?

3. What "heavy loads" were placed on converts?

4. Can you think of un-Biblical "loads" we put on new Christians?

5. What advantage was Christ's "yoke"?

6. What laws do local churches need for new converts?

7. What is your concept of the Pharisees not practicing what they taught?

9

The Rejection of Jesus

There are times in our study of the Pharisees when we are frustrated at trying to unscrew the inscrutable. Much of our material paints them as villains of the first order, and in all fairness this is the way Jesus saw the ones he dealt with. We need, though, to be reminded again that some Pharisees were noble and sincere.

Luke wrote a short account of a very peculiar conversation between the Pharisees and Jesus. It proves as baffling as any passage encountered on the subject.

"At that time some Pharisees came to Jesus and said to him, 'Leave this place and go somewhere else. Herod wants to kill you' " (Luke 13:31).

How do we consider these men who came to see Jesus? Are they a group of kind admirers who did not want to see him harmed? Or is it merely a deceptive plot to get him out of Judea?

Qualified commentators are very divided over a solution to the dilemma. With no more facts than we have, the observer is left to his own imagination to find an answer. Do we picture the entire fraternity as cut from one mold? Or do we see them as a mixed bag?

Without concrete evidence to the contrary, let us assume—and a safe assumption it is—that there were Pharisees of the highest order. There was more than one Nicodemus in Jerusalem, more than one man whose restless conscience told him that there was some truth to Christ's complaints. If there was a Pharisee who would help bury the body of Jesus, it is easy to accept the type of concern depicted in Luke chapter thirteen.

It is correct to say that the Pharisees rejected Jesus Christ. It would also be accurate to remember that Jesus rejected them and drew razor-sharp lines of demarcation.

One of Christ's more stinging contributions to this alienation was his repeated reference to them as hypocrites. Thousands of years of linguistics have never construed an uglier word for a religious person than the word *hypocrite*. It had no less acid to it then than it contains today.

The word *hypocrite* carried two meanings in the time of Christ, and he possibly intended both of them. The Hebrew concept was "godless," "lawless," or impious. The Greek word carried that same tone but added the meaning of "actor." Luke 20:20 states that the chief priest kept a close watch on Jesus and "sent spies, who pretended to be honest." When a Jew used the Greek word, he probably meant the whole ball of wax—"a godless actor." This is the meaning that has filtered down to our day and it remains accurate.

Not taking any chances of being misunderstood, Christ called the Pharisees hypocrites and then precisely defined the word by quoting Isa. 29:13.

"These people honor me with their lips,
but their hearts are far from me.
They worship me in vain;
their teachings are but rules made by men."
(Mark 7:6)

Like many modern Christians, Pharisees were shackled to a routine of religious conformity, but their faith and sincerity were an empty hull. Rom. 12:2 warns us against conformity to this world, but did not the apostle also mean religious compliance? Was it not also a cry against accepting the status quo of the church as our spiritual security?

In Matthew, Jesus outlined the basic credentials of the hypocrite. He emphasizes appearance (23:25–28); he emphasizes formalism (23:23); and he emphasizes deceit (22:18).

Some writers balk at the audacity of Christ to launch such an attack. They point out the fact that nothing was more abhorrent to a Pharisee and that he denounced hypocrisy.

Herford insists that Christ's strong teaching on honesty and sincerity did not outdo that of the rabbis. He also contends that Christ was no more relentless in renouncing hypocrisy than were his contemporaries.[1] One can only agree with these observations. Certainly there were dedicated rabbis. Certainly there were reformers who spoke out against false religion. Yet, conceding this fact does not alter another. The Pharisees to whom Jesus was speaking were hypocrites, no matter if all the other Jews in Israel were spotlessly righteous. The upstanding rabbis do not nullify the masked charlatans who also paraded the streets.

Nor do the sins of the Pharisees eradicate the fact of hypocrisy in the present-day church. It does us no service to attack the ancients if we are afraid to look in our own backyards.

One minister with a long track record said, "If our congregations knew everything we believed, none of us would be able to hold our jobs." Surely an overstatement, but possibly not too great a one. There are many things that

---

1. R. Travers Herford, *Talmud and Apocrypha* (New York: KTAV Publishing House, Inc., 1971), p. 282. (Cf. Abrahams, pt. 2, pp. 30–31.)

Christians dare not think, let alone say, or they risk ostracism.

Yet the demand for constant conformity helps tremendously to nurture this hypocrisy. Rather than feeling a free spirit to follow Christ into the daring and unknown, we are content to melt into the backdrop of a highly organized system. To this extent our credentials may be identical to those who felt Christ's darts.

It is easy to get everyone excited by the charges of hypocrisy, but, indeed, all are not guilty. There are many, like the tax collector, who cry for God to be merciful to him, a sinner. He is not pretentious and has given up trying to impress God or man with his religiosity. He knows he is incomplete. He admits his dependence on God and refuses to take on airs of haughtiness. It is not the inconsistent person who is a hypocrite; it is only the one who thinks his religious life makes him better than anyone else. Hypocrisy trades humility for spiritual arrogance.

There is considerable reason to fear "having a form of godliness but denying its power" (2 Tim. 3:5).

Jesus seems to appreciate the fact that holding hands with the Pharisees and trying to pacify them into seeing his point of view would be pointless. As with too many people who have been steeped in a religious philosophy for years, their minds had been shifted into idle and are shiftless. Therefore Christ's only alternative was open denunciation. This method might prove effective in warning the non-Pharisees and maybe even shock a few Pharisees loose. While Christ showed extreme tolerance for the less religious, here he was to follow no policy of appeasement.

It would be highly inaccurate to suggest that Jesus and the Pharisees fell out basically over personality conflicts. They were more than two irreconcilable temperaments. There were fundamental ideological differences at the root of their hostilities.

No distinction was more glaring than Jesus's claim to be the Messiah. Whether the Pharisees, scholars, or the reader believe that Jesus was the Christ, one fact is certain—Jesus said he was the Messiah, or Christ.

The high priest, in disgust over the attempts at trapping Jesus or gathering testimony against him, asked him as bluntly as he could:

"I charge you under oath by the living God: Tell us if you are the Christ, the Son of God."

"Yes, it is as you say," Jesus replied (Matt. 26:63,64).

There is also no doubt that his disciples claimed he was the Christ (for example, Andrew, John 1:41; Peter, Mark 8:29). The woman at the well in John chapter four heard Jesus apply this title to himself.

"The woman said, 'I know that Messiah (called Christ) is coming. When he comes, he will explain everything to us.' "

"Then Jesus declared, 'I who speak to you am he' " (John 4:25,26).

It is again important to try to hear as the Pharisees heard. Suppose someone stood up in church and said, "I am God's younger brother." Our reception of the gentleman would be less than overwhelming. Our passions would probably hit the Richter scale everywhere from sympathy for the poor guy to open anger.

The Pharisees were in exactly that position and all the more so because their beliefs were rigid and inflexible. They believed in the concept of a Messiah, but his precise form and manner were undecided.

The word itself is not complicated. Messiah, or the New Testament Christ, simply means "anointed one."

The Old Testament told us that God would anoint one person to be a supernatural king of the people of Israel. Slowly over the years he put the story together piece by piece.

The promise began to take shape when Jacob was on his deathbed (Gen. 49). He told Judah that one of his descendants would be a king like no other king and the people would flock around him.

Then God later dropped a big clue to David. He told the successful king, "Your family will rule my kingdom forever" (2 Sam. 7:16). He then added some large pieces of the puzzle when he gave Daniel a vision of the Son of man coming in the clouds and establishing an everlasting kingdom over all people and nations (Dan. 7:13,14). In chapter nine there appears a direct reference to an "anointed one" who will be killed (vs. 25,26).

The ancient prophet Micah added another strange note when he writes of a king who was alive from "everlasting ages past" who would be born in Bethlehem (5:2).

In the years before Jesus was born things had gone badly for the nation of Israel. Their nation was occupied by Romans and their own king had not sat on the throne for five hundred years. And yet, strangely enough, there existed a warm ray of hope among some of the people. They were reading the scriptures and hoping the Messiah would come.

The people of the Qumran community believed he would come shortly.[2] Simeon looked for a Messiah (Luke 2:26), as did the Magi (Matt. 2:2). Herod knew the story (Matt. 2:3), Andrew expected the Christ (John 1:41), as did a Samaritan woman (John 4). Who can estimate how many more had heard this story from childhood and now hoped with pining hearts that they might see him?

Some Jews thought of the concept only as a national, impersonal movement much like present-day Zionism. Others considered it all a bunch of impractical nonsense.

Support for a personal Messiah was strong among the Pharisees. Their concept may have envisioned a king leading an army and fighting for Israel's independence, but it mostly centered around a person and liberty. Other Pharisees tried

2. F. F. Bruce, *Biblical Exegesis in the Qumran Texts* (Grand Rapids: Wm. B. Eerdmans Publishing Co., 1959), p. 45.

to quell this notion lest the people get carried away over some local leader and carry the nation into bloody conflict with the Romans.

There were strong messianic feelings, especially in Galilee, and this may have led to Pilate's massacre of Galilean Passover pilgrims (Luke 13:1). Most Jews recognized the fact that the messianic hope, whatever the form it took, had to eventually find its spearhead in Jerusalem. Consequently all sorts of religions and political groups were slicing in and out of the city.[3]

This type of atmosphere was ideal for planting and cultivating messiahs. People before Christ had claimed to be the anointed one, and at least one had insisted he was born in the Davidic line.[4] Into this melee came Jesus. He stood up and said that God sent him as the Messiah and he had the credentials to prove it.

Some people looked at him and said, "Thank God." Others turned their backs and said, "Trash."

Part of the problem the Pharisees faced was not of their own making. The situation was confusing. It was easy to claim you were the Messiah, and a cartload of people had done it.

Another part of the difficulty was incubated within their own philosophy of life and religion. They thought they had all of the answers and had ceased to become learners. Their basic theology had been pigeonholed, and cement had been poured over it. Humility was not only gone but was also a sign of weakness. They had developed a steel-trap outline of how the Messiah would come, how he would appear, and what he would do. Any deviation from that pattern was obviously wrong. If it was correct, it would agree with them.

This attitude seems sinister and belligerent. That is, until we examine some of our own practices. It is easy for Chris-

3. Jeremias, op. cit., p. 75.
4. Ibid., p. 277.

tians to develop the same screw-tight views concerning the Second Coming of Christ. Some of our eschatological schemes have become so narrow and brittle that even God dare not violate them.

That may seem like an overstatement, but indeed it is very close to fact. It is discouraging to listen to tirades concerning the rapture of Christians and the events that must precede and follow the event or to read a writer who, with the precision of a clockmaker, explains where Christ will stand in which year. One is tempted to feel that if Jesus caught a bus in downtown Chicago and entered a large metropolitan church, he would be ignored or abused. Christ wasn't supposed to return that way. He might be just as summarily dismissed as he was when the Pharisees rejected him at his first coming.

Someone has said that the only thing we learn from history is that we learn nothing from history. It would be a waste to study the Pharisees and learn nothing about ourselves.

Faith with flexibility. A growing faith that is not afraid to change and turn. Faith that is open to God is a humble faith. The other kind is brittle hypocrisy.

The rejection of Jesus as the Christ was also based on similar terms that were applied to him. Those titles were "Son of man" and "Son of God."

Jesus frequently used the designation "Son of man" to describe himself. For instance, Luke 7:34: "The Son of man came eating and drinking, and you say, 'Here is a glutton and a drunk and a friend of tax collectors and sinners.' " (Also Matt. 8:20; Luke 9:22; etc.) The New Testament is replete with this phrase in reference to Jesus.

Traditionally the term had a simple meaning that denoted man's weakness in comparison to God.[5] However, Daniel's

5. Geldenhuys, op. cit., p. 352. (Cf. Lorraine Boettner, *Studies in Theology*, Grand Rapids, Mich.: William B. Eerdmans Publishing Co., 1960, p. 158.)

use of the title lifted it to paramount importance. "I saw in the night visions, and, behold, one like the Son of man came with the clouds of heaven, and came to the Ancient of days, and they brought him near before him" (Dan. 7:13 KJ).

This passage of scripture crowned the term with messianic glory. It points to heavenly origin and characteristics, and when someone had the audacity to apply it to himself, eyebrows rose like venetian blinds. There can be no doubt that Jesus very consciously applied the messianic title to himself.

Some observers feel that Jesus could not really have said these words about himself. They insist that his natural humility would have prohibited such a boast. However, his meekness did not destroy his honesty. If he knew he was the Son of man, that is, Messiah, his very mission demanded he announce it. Otherwise it would be like Dr. Salk burying his vaccine out of shyness.

The second title was equally devastating as far as the Pharisees were concerned. The "Son of God" is frequently used in the New Testament; in fact, John explains that the very reason he wrote his gospel was so man would "believe that Jesus is the Christ, the Son of God" (20:31). While we debate what this term meant, we should remember that there was no confusion among the Jews. They very bluntly accused Jesus of blasphemy for applying the term to himself. Jesus in return admits that he has called himself exactly that (John 10:22–39). Messiah is an interchangeable term with "Son of God," with special emphasis on his filial relationship with God.

This peculiar origin with God appears to be in the guard's mind when Christ is executed. He, a Gentile pagan, remarks, "Surely this man was the Son of God" (Mark 15:39).

One can appreciate the fact that these terms caused the Pharisees to jump up and down, but not with joy. They never would have been compatible. If they had not wanted to kill him before, surely this form of blasphemy was intolerable.

To his sympathizers the evidence for his messiahship was abundant. Many people, including John the Baptist, testified to his qualifications. Pains were taken to demonstrate his Davidic line. He performed the miracles and ministered to the poor as the Messiah was supposed to. However, for all of this it still needed the paste of faith to hold it together. If a person did not choose to believe, then no one could force him to accept it.

Unconvinced that Jesus was the prince come from heaven, the Pharisees believed his princely stature came from another direction. As he was healing the blind and the mute and casting out demons, the crowds exclaimed, "Could this be the Son of David?"

"But when the Pharisees heard this they said, 'It is only by Beelzebub, the prince of demons, that this fellow drives out demons' " (Matt. 12:22–24).

While they may have found him intriguing, they could not find him enticing. Many of them could have talked at length of their enthusiastic anticipation of the coming Messiah, and yet he may have walked past the drawn shades of their minds.

Many of us can appreciate the search for ultimate and unchanging truth. There is tremendous security in having all of the answers sorted out. Indeed, the person who is very sure of himself is the envy of many around him. But if the price of security is a closed mind, it may be too great a rate.

Maybe Jesus will return in the clouds, and Christians will be suddenly and neatly extracted from earth. Maybe Christ will return at the head of a heavenly army breaking the strength of a godless army. And then again our interpretations may be entirely inaccurate and he is presently working as a stevedore in Baltimore.

Certainly the latter description can't be true. We all know

our Bible too well to accept that. But then the Pharisees felt the same way and decided to crucify that madman.

The man without a humble spirit is powerless to interpret the Bible. The person with a spiritual strut poses the worst form of hypocrisy, even while he denies it.

Questions for Further Thought

1. What were Pharisees trying to do to Christ in Luke 13:31?

2. Give your personal definition of a hypocrite.

3. Where did the Pharisees get the idea that Jesus claimed to be the Messiah?

4. Find the Old Testament hints of a Messiah.

5. Why were the Pharisees unable to accept Jesus as the Messiah?

6. What were the implications behind the title "Son of man"?

7. What lesson does the rejection by the Pharisees have for us?

10
Overcome by Hate

For almost twenty centuries the Jewish people have taken a terrible amount of abuse over the death of Christ. Many have been taunted since childhood as "Christ-killers," many have been hunted down, and many have been murdered. It is probably impossible for any Gentile to understand the enormous suffering they have experienced.

We hear astronomical figures like "six million Jews killed in World War II," but that doesn't begin to tell the story. Large numbers of their executioners have always been church members. Some turned their backs and refused to watch the murders and others held the guns, set the fires, and tied the ropes.

If it is a wonder to some Christians why so few Jews are converted, it is an amazement to others that any Jews are. From massive atrocities like the Spanish Inquisition to the individual horrors of Alfred Dreyfus and Leo Frank, the Jews have suffered terribly.

It is true that the New Testament teaches that the Jews were instrumental in the death of Christ. However, what sort of demented mentality makes all Jews responsible for the execution? An actor with Southern sympathies killed Lincoln, and yet we don't label all actors who like the South as "Lincoln-killers."

There were some men who were Jews who sought to kill Jesus. There were some Romans who killed Jesus. There are some of us who, had we been alive, might have wanted to kill Jesus too. It is nonsense to say that the Jews as a nation murdered Jesus. People killed Christ, and if we had been alive, we might have been among them.

In this chapter we do not flinch from the facts that certain Pharisees and Herodians, led by Caiaphas and carried out by the coward Pilate, were the main characters in the Crucifixion. However, it was a mentality, a way of thinking, a degenerate nature that allowed them to do it, and it did not take Christians very long to adopt a similar murderous logic.

It is fairly simple to trace the thinking process that led up to arrest and execution. The Pharisees considered plotting, trickery, and deceit as acceptable modes of operation for the religious leaders of Israel.

Many of the questions that the Pharisees asked Jesus were not for the purpose of examining him. They had made up their minds early that he was not the Christ or any other of God's relatives. Now they were trading barbs in hope of making the crowds see what a fraud he was.

The exchange over divorce was not to gather information but rather to allienate Christ's audience. They knew how divided the people were on the subject, so they tested or pulled at Christ (Matt. 19:3). They realized what the Scriptures said about the greatest commandment, but they asked to see if he would differ from it (Matt. 22:35). In case there is any doubt of their intentions and what *test* or *tempt* means, look at the interpretation that Jesus gives to their questions.

When the Pharisees and Herodians asked him about paying taxes to Caesar, they first gave him a list of insincere compliments. They said he was a man of integrity and a teacher of God who was not swayed by the opinions of men; then they laid the bomb on him.

"Tell us, then, what is your opinion? Is it right to pay taxes to Caesar or not?"

"But Jesus, knowing their evil intent, said, 'You hypocrites, why are you trying to trap me?' " (Matt. 22:17–18).

Christ went on to answer the question, but he was not fooled about their actual intentions. They could not stand to hear the things he said, but they might have been able to ignore that if it had not been for those terrible crowds. Both John the Baptist and Jesus were drawing congregations of ten thousand, and people were beginning to take them seriously. Consequently they had to find a solution to the "Jesus problem."

In the Gospel account it is easy to see a plan begin to formulate. After Jesus healed the shriveled hand in the synagogue on a Sabbath, they became furious and started to discuss "what they might do with Jesus" (Luke 6:11). After Christ healed the thirty-eight-year-old invalid, he was given the same warm reception because the man carried his mat on the Sabbath. "For this reason the Jews tried all the harder to kill him" (John 5:18). Their intentions were not lost on Jesus, and eventually he started avoiding Judea because he knew the contract was out to kill (John 7:1).

It has been said that those who are capable of loving very deeply are also capable of hating just as deeply. Many religious people confuse sincerity with fanaticism. Sincerity deals with dedication and commitment. Fanaticism affects our judgment and behavior, causing us to do things that are absurd and contrary to our better instincts.

Fanaticism caused Christians to torture and exterminate Jews who would not be converted during the Inquisition. It sent William the Conqueror against the equally fanatic Turks, and both sides killed for their "faith." It is easy to see why the nonreligious are reluctant to become involved in worship that often seems to only harden hearts rather than make them tender.

The same Jewish faith had spawned immense acts of charity and promoted a highly moral monotheism. Now men were twisting it in order to give birth to immoral behavior.

Using murders as a solution to their problems was not isolated to the case of Jesus. Frustrated and angry, they were prone to lunge out with force to correct what they could not cope with. No incident was more devastating to them than the resurrection of Lazarus. Of all the miracles none was more embarrassing to the Pharisees than for witnesses to see the Nazarene raise a man who had been in the grave for four days.

When people started responding to the news, they began to find Jesus very appealing and extremely credible. Bursting with tension and unable to explain or accept the resurrection, the chief priests decided to destroy the evidence and rekill Lazarus.

"So the chief priests made plans to kill Lazarus as well, for on account of him many of the Jews were going over to Jesus and putting their faith in him" (John 12:10,11).

Technically, the Sanhedrin was responsible for the decision to kill Jesus. It was not the result of mob action but the calculating decision of an official ruling body within Jerusalem.

The Sanhedrin was the supreme Jewish council, which was given the authority of local legislative and judiciary functions among the Jews. Just how much power they had at any given time depended on how much the ruling king and governor wanted them to have.

The main group consisted of seventy-one members, and there were two smaller ones of lower power numbering twenty-three each. The Jews believed that the organization had its roots from the time when Moses selected seventy men to help him organize approximately one million people (Num. 11:10–24). Later Ezra collected a similar group of assistants.

From the point of view of Herod and the Romans, the Sanhedrin was very helpful. It made it easier to rule Israel if Jewish leaders would take care of the daily matters and leave kings and governors to do whatever kings and governors do.

The high priest, in this case Caiaphas, and sometimes Annas, presided over the body. The members consisted of a mixture of Sadducees and Pharisees. According to Josephus, the Pharisees had heavy influence on the Sanhedrin because they represented views of the populace at large. While the Sadducees often disagreed, they maintained a healthy respect and knew when to back off.[1]

The Sadducees had no truck with the Pharisees' picky little codes and traditional laws. They considered themselves more conservative because they held more strictly to the Old Testament alone. They even considered the Pharisaic view of the resurrection to be an invention and aberration. They represented an aristocratic thinking and were very popular among the wealthy class.[2] They did not make friends with Jesus either (Matt. 16:12).

The men of the Sanhedrin met in deliberate discourse and weighed the evidence of the relentless Christ. The president and convenor (Caiaphas), a Sadducee and high priest presided. The issue at stake was that "the whole world has gone after him," and what can they do with Jesus.

Caiaphas was well aware of the precarious political posture. If King Herod chose to, he could depose the high priest at any moment, and high priests were changed often. If

---

1. Josephus, *Antiquities*, trans. William Whiston (Grand Rapids, Mich.: Kregel Publications, 1969), 18.1.4.
2. Jeremias, op. cit., p. 228.

the crowds became large and threatening, the Romans would become suspicious of an insurrection and send storm troopers into Palestine to lop off heads. They then might choose to scatter the Jews throughout the empire.

The job of the Sanhedrin was clear-cut. Caiaphas needed to rule the internal matters of Palestine efficiently and quietly. Consequently Caiaphas takes on a role of heroic proportions. While many Christians sneer at his name today, his decision was popular at the time and received wide support both from the Sanhedrin and from the general populace (Matt. 27:22).

One has to be intrigued about the discussion that took place in the council. We know for a fact that one man dissented with the decision, and a second may have.

The first person was Joseph of Arimathea, and the Gospel account clearly tells us that he was "a good and upright man, who had not consented to their decision and action" (Luke 23:50,51). One can only imagine the raw courage it would have taken for a secret disciple to disagree in that emotionally charged meeting. The very hesitancy must have bordered on treason. His later action in claiming the body of Christ demonstrated one of history's finest moments of reluctant bravery.

Nicodemus may have been the second dissenting voice, but we cannot be certain. He had held a private audience with Jesus and afterward defended Jesus before the Pharisees. "Does our law condemn a man without first hearing him to find out what he is doing?" (John 7:51). For this mild complaint he was accused of being a Galilean. Strengthened by what he saw, this Pharisee chose to join Joseph and rescue the body of Christ.

Whatever resistance may have been offered, the effect was similar to a man standing on a track to try and stop a train. Except for the faintest thud, the project went on without interruption.

Not only in this story but also throughout life one has to be amazed at the religious man's potential for crass hate. That hate becomes all the more reprehensible when he claims that love motivates him to hate. Consequently, a man announces that he loves God so much that he is willing to murder someone who does not love the same God. History is crowded with people who have done exactly that.

Jesus warned his disciples that perverted love would turn into acid and eat away at man. These men will attend worship services before they turn to kill their fellowman. Indeed, he said, ". . . a time is coming when anyone who kills you will think he is offering a service to God" (John 16:2).

The problem becomes even more bewildering when people of the same basic religious persuasions turn on each other. We find Baptists intolerant of Presbyterians or Catholics carrying grudges against Orthodox. One must conclude that many people have missed the essential ingredients. They have baked a cake without flour; they have served a pie without filling.

Men still scratch their head at the teaching of Jesus on the subject, but his observations were not so unfair. He told us that the person who hates his neighbor stands in judgment just as surely as the one who murders (Matt. 5:43). A strict and difficult standard but a necessary one. If we are to control our actions, we must first be able to arrest our emotions.

Even more dangerous than the man who hates is the person who hates and denies it at the same time. Christians realize that they should not hate and yet they find themselves doing it. Morally embarrassed at such a debased attitude, they often attempt to cover it up by giving it another name, such as "indignation." Then they may try to disguise their true actions by saying that they only hate him "to help him." However, a new vocabulary and an agile rationale do not remove the basic fact that Christians often operate out of an unadulterated hate.

The Pharisees also had their sane moments, and none was more noble than that of Gamaliel as he is described in Acts, chapter five. Gamaliel was a teacher of the first order who at one time had Paul of Tarsus as a pupil (Acts 22:3). His reputation as an instructor-philosopher-theologian was so excellent that someone later wrote that reverence for the law, and purity and abstinence died with him.[3]

He was the grandson of the famous Rabbi Hillel and the first person to receive the title "Rabban," which means "Our Great One," rather than ordinary "Rabbi." As with many other Pharisees, he tried to make fair observations and gentle judgments.

When the apostles preached the death, burial, and resurrection of Jesus, the Sanhedrin became even angrier and wanted to put them to death (Acts 5:33), but Gamaliel suggested a mediating position, "Leave these men alone! Let them go! For if their purpose or activity is of human origin, it will fail. But if it is from God, you will not be able to stop these men; you will only find yourself fighting against God" (Acts 5:38,39).

However, in this case Gamaliel's voice became only another sparrow's cry lost in the storm. While they were persuaded for the moment, they arose again to kill Christians in an attempt to quell this new cult.

Paul (or Saul) took up the gauntlet and made the persecution a personal crusade against those who disagreed. Paul was a member of the Pharisees and remained very proud of the fact. They were a strict sect, and he had felt that their standards had been good for him. This zeal for religion took him to the ultimate extreme. It is a high degree when a man will give his life for his faith. Yet it seems an even greater fanaticism that will allow a man to kill another person for

3. F. F. Bruce, *The Book of Acts* (Grand Rapids: Wm. B. Eerdmans, 1960).

God, faith, and church. Paul had entered that severe circle of those who would murder because they loved.

He traveled the countryside hunting out men and women who called themselves Christians (or members of "The Way") and brought them prisoner to Jerusalem to be tried (Acts 9:1,2). It would be difficult to exaggerate what persecution he leveled on local believers. However, Luke writes that after Paul's conversion "the church throughout Judea, Galilee and Samaria enjoyed a time of peace" (Acts 9:31).

The stoning of Stephen has all of the earmarks of being not the clumsy work of an unwieldy crowd but rather the work of an official Old Testament execution. *The Interpreter's Dictionary of the Bible*[4] notes the similarities as they are outlined in Lev. 24:14 and Deut. 17:7. Witnesses were sought, and he was interrogated. They took him outside of the town to be stoned, and the witnesses cast the first stones. While the execution was carried out, a young man named Saul stood by giving his consent to the deed.

Rather than the concept of a spontaneous and outraged crowd, we need to see the Sanhedrin functioning in official session again.[5] However, it was soon evident that one murder would only lead to another, and the disciples of Christ would not be easily exterminated.

After Paul's conversion he found himself standing on strange ground before the Sanhedrin. After exciting a crowd because of preaching the Good News of Jesus Christ, a Roman soldier took him before the council to find out what in the world was going on. To the Sanhedrin Paul defended the fact that he was proud to be a Pharisee and that he was being tried only because like they, he believed in the resurrection.

4. Vol. 4, p. 218.
5. Ibid., pp. 169ff.

In one of the odd events of history some of the Pharisees started agreeing with Paul and demanded he be set free. "We find nothing wrong with this man," they said. "What if a spirit or an angel has spoken to him?" (Acts 23:9). The discussion became so heated and violent that the Roman escort had to call in troops to rescue Paul from the angry religious leaders.

Despite the hostilities and even murders, there is quite another side to the Pharisaic reaction. The vast majority probably never developed any feelings on the subject to exceed cool apathy. All of them doubtless heard of the new cult and its dead leader, but they didn't get too excited one way or the other. A second group was sizzling hot. Yet there was also a third group emerging and growing that felt that maybe Jesus was what he claimed to be. This segment entered the local churches complete with all of their strengths and accompanying conflicts.

A large part of the tragedy that was their story was as human as love and laughter. Some of them allowed their better judgment to become completely clouded by their intense hate. This is not to imply that if they had sat down in the shade of any evening and thought this through calmly, the Pharisees would have lined up to become Christians. Only the most naive believe that faith is a matter of calculation alone and that any normal logic will conclude that the Church is irresistible.

However, we do suggest that if men had not surrendered to base passions they could have avoided the horrible decision of killing Christians. But then the resistance of prejudices and hatred would have saved millions of people all over the world throughout history.

The murdering of innocent people will probably continue all over the world as long as religious people consider hate to be an acceptable life-style.

Paul had served in both capacities in life, as the hater and as the hated, and he wrote:

"If it is possible, as far as it depends on you, live at peace with everyone. Do not take revenge my friends, but leave room for God's wrath, for it is written: It is mine to avenge, I will repay, says the Lord. On the contrary, if your enemy is hungry, feed him; if he is thirsty, give him something to drink" (Rom. 12:18–20).

Christians have never had a greater enemy than hate.

Questions for Further Thought

1. Is there an anti-Jewish feeling among the Christians you know? How would you describe the attitude?

2. In your opinion, why have Christians persecuted Jews?

3. Can you suggest ways to build bridges between Jews and Christians?

4. Explain the Pharisaic attitude toward the resurrected Lazarus?

5. Do the Christians you know hate more, less, or the same as the non-Christians? Explain.

6. Can you think of an example of a Christian who successfully resisted hate?

7. How can the church teach a proper handling of normal emotions?

11
The Big Show

What is the point of living a righteous life if no one knows about it? After all, the only thing more important than being humble is to look humble. This is the philosophy that the Pharisees either knowingly or unknowingly adopted. As they moved into this compartment, they were joined by many of us who reluctantly employ the same principles.

Two of the most obvious badges of piety worn by the Pharisees were phylacteries and tassels. Jesus Christ told them, "Everything they do is done for men to see: they make their phylacteries wide and the tassels of their prayer shawls long; they love the place of honor at banquets and the most important seats in the synagogues; they love to be greeted in the market places and to have men call them 'Rabbi'" (Matt. 23:5-7).

The entire question of phylacteries began with an honest attempt to interpret two verses in Exodus, chapter thirteen. Verses nine and sixteen state, "It shall be a sign unto thee upon thine hands, and for a memorial between their eyes." To many people the passage is a figure of speech; but to others, such as the Pharisees, they took it quite literally and decided to place parts of the Word of God on their arm and forehead.

A phylactery was a little leather case into which four scriptural passages were placed (Exod. 13:1–10; Exod. 13:11–16; Deut. 6:4–9; Deut. 11:13–21), and the box was tied to the left arm. The leather case was made from a clean animal. The black leather strap by which it was fastened was wound seven times around the arm and three times around the hand.

The box itself was difficult to see since it was placed on the inside of the arm so that the scriptures would be close to the heart. These boxes are in modern times called tephillin or tefillin, the plural and singular being the same.

The second box was placed high on the forehead at the base of the hairline. This box had four compartments, and each section contained a slip of parchment with one of the four scriptural passages written on it. Each of these was tied with a well-washed hair from a calf's tail. They were afraid wool or thread could hold a fungus growth and thus pollute them.[1]

It may be true that Christ does not condemn the wearing of the phylactery, but he certainly is dismayed that they would widen them so they would be more noticeable. He was concerned at their promotion of what Barclay calls "a religion of ostentation."[2]

There may be some who are tempted to accuse Christ of being picky. If they want to wear these little trinkets and it helps their faith, why not leave them alone? But give Christ more credit than that. He knew what they really were and he knew what they were likely to become.

There is no doubt that it became a good-luck charm for many Israelites. In fact, the Greek word means "amulet" or "charm," and many Jews felt they had God's particular protection when they wore the tefillin.[3] As late as the twelfth century Maimonides felt the same way, "But he who is ac-

1. Robertson, op. cit., vol. 1, pp. 178ff.
2. Barclay, op cit., vol. 2, p. 316.
3. Josephus, *Antiquities*, 4.8.13.

customed to wear tefillin will live long, as it is written 'When the Lord is with them, they will live.' "

Many Jews still use them today, beginning at their Bar Mitzvah when they reach the age of thirteen. Women are not allowed to wear a tefillin.

It is not unusual for superstition to mix with religion until the two are hard to separate and identify. It is easy to find people who believe that things are going badly for them and their family because they have not done certain religious routines. Too soon we forget that the rain falls on both the righteous and the unrighteous.

God becomes merely a genie, and if we rub his lantern in the right manner, he will be released and give us whatever we want. If we are not careful, even daily devotions will degenerate into a four-leaf clover. Rather than using meditation as a communication with God that is healthy, it may become a rabbit's foot stroked regularly to promote our success.

Once the phylactery or tefillin got going well, a series of theological laws surrounded it for support. In the sixteenth-century code the Shulchan Aruch there are 160 laws listed for its regulation and use. There were some ancient Jews who taught that when we meet God, he will be wearing a tefillin.

There was a story that if a person did not have time to study the Torah, God would say, "Perform the commandment concerning tefillin and I will consider that as if you had been studying the Torah night and day." [4]

Traditionally, the tefillin was to be worn for morning prayers only, and it is used in this way today. However, the Pharisees turned them into a parade; they wore them more often and enlarged them to make sure they were properly acknowledged by everyone.

It is true that Jesus does not condemn the tefillin as such.

4. Ausubel, op. cit., pp. 458–59.

Frankly, we do not know if he took those Old Testament passages literally. We do know that in the several references to his prayer sessions there is no mention of these devices. His complaint was definitely in the fact that people would enlarge them so that others would be impressed with their righteousness. Christ did not consider such "showing off" to be righteousness at all.

The second section of Christ's objection in Matt. 23:5 concerned making the "tassels of their prayer shawls long." As usual, the basic practice had a good Biblical foundation.

"The Lord said to Moses, 'Tell the people of Israel to make tassels for the hems of their clothes (this is a permanent regulation from generation to generation) and to attach the tassels to their clothes with a blue cord. The purpose of this regulation is to remind you, whenever you notice the tassels, of the commandments of the Lord, that you are to obey his laws instead of following your own desires and going your own ways, as you used to do in serving other gods" (Num. 15:37–39).

These were worn on the four corners of the outer garment and later moved to the inner clothing. This then became part of the prayer shawl that devout Jews wear on certain occasions even to this day.

As with the phylacteries, Jesus has no complaint to this point concerning their interpretation of the custom. Some people insist that Christ wore one, which may well be the case. Those promoting this theory feel that the woman who wanted to touch Christ's garment and knew she would be healed (Matt. 9:20) pointed to a superstition that it held mystical powers. This view is highly speculative; however, there may be some truth to the notion.

Christ's objection to this centered only on the exaggerated size of the tassels. The original purpose was to remind the wearer of God not to be a billboard to announce your reported holiness to the public.

Their peculiar emphasis qualified the Pharisees as the great-grandfather of the "how do we look" cult. But while they may get credit for being famous founding fathers, they may well have been outdone by their Christian siblings. The necessity to keep up appearances may have so permeated Christianity as to leave it extremely sterile out of fear of looking bad.

Consequently many Christians make great efforts to make sure they attend religious functions lest people begin to wonder if they are "slipping." Some carry their Bibles because they want to study them, while others tote them as a "testimony" to their piety. Others are convinced that the neat, close-cut hair style serves as evidence that they have not rebelled against God.

A local church discusses the practicality of closing their Wednesday-night service in favor of a more fruitful approach. Would Christ have been just as dismayed to hear the members object because of what people would think? After all, the lights would be off in the building, and other people would think we are giving up the faith.

Dr. Paul Tournier has made some excellent remarks concerning the children raised in this type of atmosphere (*The Person Reborn*). Some of them have tremendous difficulties relating to God because their early exposure was one of continuously asking, "Well, how would that look?" rather than the kernel questions of the Christian life.

Part of the modern problem had the same innocent beginning as the Pharisees experienced. The contortion began in the misapplication of several passages of scripture. For instance, 1 Thess. 5:22, where the King James translates the verse: "Abstain from all appearances of evil." To many this seemed clear enough. Anything that looked evil to anyone was to be avoided because we would not look sufficiently holy. Consequently there was a tendency to withdraw from anything that looked "worldly" and an added emphasis on things that appeared to be righteous.

The difficulty with this verse and others like it is that it is both an incorrect translation and even a worse application. *The New International Version* renders it: "Avoid every kind of evil." *The Living Bible* agrees with the meaning and writes: "Keep away from every kind of evil." The correct emphasis focuses on the *evil* and not on the *appearance*. Jesus walked with tax collectors, prostitutes, and Samaritans because he refused to be concerned over "how do I look?" It is hard to imagine that if Jesus walked our streets today, he would be afraid to enter a bar. But how would that look? And Jesus might reply, "That's your hang-up. I have more important questions to ask."

This philosophy is ingrained in some Christians no less deeply than it was among the Pharisees. There are many Christians who refuse to believe that 1 Thess. 5:22 can be translated any other way except in the King James fashion or interpreted other than in modern dogma. They are the losers, because while they laugh at the absurdity of the Pharisees, they have in fact outdone them in their narrowness.

There is a word that comes from the Greek and describes a large reason why some Christians are paralyzed in their abuses. *Xenophobia* comes from the word *xenos* (pronounced *zenos*) meaning "strange, foreign, or different." It means that someone is afraid of something that is new or strange. The Pharisees had closed their box on knowledge and thoroughly resented anyone who tried to pry open the lid and introduce anything foreign or new. Too many modern Christians have their beliefs and practices stored neatly in little pigeonholes, and they would resent it if even God tried to shake up that filing system. Jesus Christ dared to disrupt it, and his boldness proved to be a one-way street to the cross.

This very "show-off" syndrome is elaborated on in the latter part of the paragraph in Matt. 23:5-7. When the Pharisees attended the banquets, they were very touchy about getting positions of honor, where they could be recognized and appreciated.

In their time this meant being placed at the head of a table in a reclining position where one could see and be seen easily. Throughout Israel's vast history they ate in many different styles; however, during the time of Christ reclining on divans or couches was much in vogue. Wide couches were often placed on three sides of the table leaving the fourth side for servants to accommodate the guests.

It is evident that the Christian disciples fared just as poorly at this game as did the Pharisees. Note James and John arguing over where they might sit in the kingdom to come (Mark 10:37). Then read how Christ expects a person to humble himself even at prestigious gatherings (Luke 14:7-11) and reminds his followers that the really important people at a banquet are those who wait on tables, because they have learned to serve (Luke 22:24-30).

Then he turns his quick attention to those who march into the synagogues like parade floats that have escaped from the Rose Bowl. Jeremias tells us that there were special seats of honor at the front of the synagogue, as strange as this may sound to some of us.[5] The leading Pharisees sat in these seats facing the congregation with their back to the cupboard holding the Torah. The back seats were reserved for children and rather unimportant worshipers.

The implications of Jesus denouncing this type of behavior become staggering for the present-day Christians and their clergy. If there is even a temptation for us to feel superior to the first-century charlatans, examples such as this should wake us up sharply. What does it say to the local congrega-

5. Jeremias, op. cit., p. 244.

tion that searches after the banker to help lead our "ecclesiastical corporation"? What does it say about our preoccupation with Christian movie stars, football players, and politicians, who may be placed on a pedestal far above the gas-station attendant, housewife, and mailman? What, indeed, does it say about introducing visiting ministers or missionaries on Sunday morning and displaying them *ad nauseam*?

One short generation after Christ's ministry the local church was still having trouble because they were easily impressed by "important" people. That is why James had to confront the early believers about their favoritism. When wealthy men entered the meeting, their gold rings and fine clothing immediately hypnotized everyone, and they got the best seats in the house. When the poor arrived, they were scooted into any clumsy corner (James 2:1-4).

There is a story concerning a governor of California who reportedly visited a Presbyterian Church. As he and his entourage were ushered into the sanctuary, one man hurried ahead and politely asked a couple to move out of the third row. As the minister watched from the platform, he could see what was about to happen and moved swiftly down into the aisle. Taking the man gently by the arm, he explained that, "We don't do that here." The governor sat wherever there was room and, to his credit, thereafter made it his home church.

The Pharisees are our not-too-distant cousins. They have done very little that we have not worked hard to match in action or in spirit. We have used them as whipping posts when in fact they make better mirrors. But then, if we can give them a going over, it takes the attention off ourselves.

Once having sounded this note against window-dressing faith, Jesus does not lay it down quickly. He goes on to describe the Pharisees as a putrid cup. Imagine that we ate our breakfast of hot cereal in a large soup cup; then without cleaning it, our wife served us vegetable-beef stew for lunch in the same vessel. Then evening brings a dessert of chocolate pudding on top of the previous stain and leftovers. Yet before each meal the outside of the cup has been scrubbed meticulously. By the time we get our oats the next morning in that same raunchy cup, its rancid odor may send us into pain.

That is the terrible accusation Christ made against the Pharisees (Matt. 23:25), and do not think for a moment that they were too dull to catch its full force. He called them blind and hypocrites, two phrases not appreciated by anyone, but especially loathed by those who claim to be spiritually aware.

Then, without flinching, he likened them to whitewashed tombs. They were familiar with the term and the practice. During the Passover season many travelers came to Jerusalem, passing the many tombstones that dotted the roadside. Since a Jew was not allowed to touch neither anything dead nor a grave (Num. 19:16) because if he did, he would be defiled for seven days, the people in the community would whiten the tombstones with a powdered lime dust so that people could avoid them. This is the type Christ was talking about, and he uses a word that means dust or lime. The rock-hewn tombs of the well-to-do were actually whitewashed a month before Passover. His illustration was not exaggerated but was a well-known idiom with plenty of examples all around.

Jesus flunked another lesson in how to win friends, but then he wasn't out to win that degree anyway. As we read it, we are usually dispassionate and academic about the charges. However, to appreciate the scene, imagine that someone was standing face to face with us and saying, "You are a phony, a hypocrite, and a dud." What would that do to our boiling point? How would it affect our disposition? It affected the Pharisees the exact same way. And Jesus wanted it to.

One has to wonder if much of the present religious activity is not a cover for the same rigor mortis. By keeping busy, we can elude any temptation to think seriously. By being light on our feet, we sidestep the challenge to "Be still and know that I am God." Therefore, some Christians would rather build a subway of commotion than sit down and invite God to quietly help our hearts.

For ten years I served as a pastor. Part of that time I organized, promoted, and prodded as much program as could be compiled. Then, seeing the fruitlessness and emptiness of the hummingbird approach to the Christian life, I decided to try to turn that ship around. It would have been easier to reverse the wind bare-handed.

The fact is that most Christians seem to thrive on hyperactivity. They may complain about the extra choir rehearsals, the Saturday-morning play practice, the business meetings, and the Christian-education committee, but try to eliminate them and we quickly discover how much the people really love them. Just like a popular mouthwash, they hate meetings twice a day.

Is it indelicate to suggest that it is easier to put on a show than it is to sit and listen to our conscience? Is it crude to question our motives in moving out on the racetrack of religious madness?

Jesus Christ was just that indelicate and precisely that crude. His words to the Pharisees were not exactly a Mack Sennett comedy. He wanted to help both the Pharisees and those whom they affected, and if waving the red flag was the best way, then break it out.

In the Sermon on the Mount, Christ took a swipe at people who blew trumpets when they gave to the poor (Matt. 6:2-4). It is unlikely that Jesus ever saw any literally blow a trumpet to call the poor together, and assuredly it was not done in the synagogues.[6] Nevertheless, he got the point across by hyperbole. Don't make such a big show about your religious exercises lest you prove to be just a blowhard.

In doing this, the Messiah issued a call; a commission, if you will. A call to the inconspicuous, a call to the unpretentious, a call to service, a call to humility, a call to personal dedication as opposed to an unconscious participation in a circus.

Questions for Further Thought

1. How did phylacteries begin?

2. What superstitions have been connected with them?

3. Are there superstitions connected with present-day Christianity?

4. Are we part of the "how do we look" cult? If so, does it affect our children?

5. Explain the problem of 1 Thess. 5:22.

6. Do church activities help or retard the personal Christian life?

7. What does the Pharisees' desire for prominence at banquets and in synagogues suggest to us today?

6. R. C. H. Lenski, *The Interpretation of St. Matthew's Gospel* (Columbus, Ohio: The Wartburg Press, 1951), p. 256.

12
Moral Policemen

During a three-year period Jesus and the Pharisees battled over practically everything but acne. Yet with the possible exception of his messiahship, no friction rubbed hotter than the question of keeping the Sabbath.

It would be difficult to overstate the hatred caused by their differences on this subject. The best summary comes from the account of Christ healing a shriveled hand on the Sabbath. After exchanging some heated words over the miracle, "the Pharisees went out and plotted how they might kill Jesus," Matthew tells us (12:14).

The Sabbath meant that much to some of the Pharisees, and they insisted it bear the same weight on everyone else. They fell into the same trap as many religious extremists. They considered themselves not only the guardians of their own souls but also the moral policemen for everyone. It is a traditional role, which demands that its scruples be observed, and they were willing to use legal leverage or even physical force to enforce their views.

Too much of Christianity long ago accepted this same rationale. They not only adopted the moral-policemen mentality, but also many to this day both accept it and even demand it. It is the same thinking that did not shop on Sundays so it made such shopping illegal. It is the same passion that distrusted long hair on men and consequently declared it immoral.

A gentlemen from South Africa spoke at a Rotary Club and said that one church in his country prided itself in controlling people. If someone from that church mowed his lawn on Sunday, he could count on a visit from his minister on Monday to reprimand him. In America some pastors will call on those who miss Sunday-evening services or will even remove a Sunday-school teacher who attends the movies.

Helpfulness too soon degenerates into power, which degenerates into a sham. One must appreciate the warning of the Southern Baptist A. T. Robertson, who reminds us that we have fallen into the same web as the Pharisees. As he wrote: The church was made for man and not man for the church.

Christ and the Pharisees hit head on with a bang comparable to two cars colliding on the highway. They discuss the "problem" of the Sabbath on seven different occasions. Five of the debates center around Christ healing on the Sabbath: a shriveled hand, a bowed back, dropsy, an invalid, and a blind man. The other two instances are when his disciples picked grain and in response to a question.

It is interesting that these two opinions both began from the same source. Moses carried the Ten Commandments, which taught man to set aside the Sabbath for rest (Exod. 20:8–11). The differences arose from trying to interpret that simple principle.

Many Jews agreed with Jesus. More than once the rabbis said the Sabbath was given for people and not people for the Sabbath.[1] Even the contemporary of Christ, Hillel, was rescued in a snow storm on the Sabbath, and he agreed that the laws were suspended when life was endangered. Life was more sacred than the law.

1. Herford, op. cit., pp. 115–17.

Jesus went further and insisted that not only was life more sacred but likewise health and kindness were also more important. If a law prevented someone from helping a needy neighbor, then something was wrong with the law.

One famous account, recorded in all three Synoptics, tells of Christ and his followers walking through a grain field when a few of his disciples picked some of the wheat or barley (Matt. 12, Mark 2, Luke 6). Their action was clearly not thievery since the Old Testament allowed this privilege to travelers.

The Pharisees, watching them, created a ruckus immediately. They felt that picking grain and rubbing it in one's hands constituted threshing and was clearly immoral. They recognized the right to do this if one was starving, but the disciples were hardly on the brink of extinction.

Jesus replied, in defense of his men, that no lesser a figure than the renowned David had eaten sacred bread from the temple, which normally was forbidden, and the king also shared some with his associates.

What Christ was saying did not fall on deaf ears. Not only did he defend his right to take the grain but he also made an analogy between himself and King David. The frequent comparisons added to the discomfort of the Pharisees.

Then, in case any of them were dense, he said, "So the Son of man is Lord even of the Sabbath" (Mark 2:28).

His reason, then, for picking grain on the Sabbath was twofold. One, it helped man; and two, as the Messiah he was in an excellent position to make the best use of the Sabbath.

Both ancient and modern scholars have insisted that Jesus made clumsy mistakes in this setting. Some feel that it was inexcusable that the disciples did not prepare their food on Friday. They also believe he was in error in relaxing the laws concerning travel, rescue, and food.[2]

Yet for Christ, when laws prohibited compassion, the laws

2. Abrahams, op. cit., pt. 1, pp. 129ff.

were being misapplied. Laws were heartless unless they contained the warmth of human love.

It reminds one of the young man who had only recently became a Christian. Some of his newly acquired moral-police friends told him he couldn't play cards because they were satanic. His aged grandmother loved to play canasta, and he said, "No one can tell me that playing cards with my lonely grandmother is satanic."

The laws that God provided never lost sight of people. The laws that men make are putrid when they become an end in themselves. Three cheers for a system that can assist lonely people. There can be only contempt for a system that expects people to serve it.

The dastardly effects of an airtight mentality can be seen clearly when Christ healed the shriveled hand on another Sabbath (Mark 3:1-6). The passage says that the moral policemen had perched like vultures watching a stray calf stagger across the desert. If it starts to stumble, they are ready to sweep down and pounce on its weakened carcass.

But Jesus refused to be intimidated by the convoy of condors. With remarkable flare, he asked the man to stand up in front of everyone. Then he threw out a rhetorical question, "Which is lawful on the Sabbath: to do good or to do evil, to save life or to kill?" No answer came from the gallery and no answer was necessary. Had the Pharisee Hillel been there, he probably would have cheered Jesus on to heal the man because he emphasized the positive on the Sabbath. If Shammai had been there, he might have hoped Jesus would back off since he dwelt on what man could not do.

Jesus was probably angry on a number of occasions, but it is interesting that this is the only passage that unequivocally says he looked at them "in anger." Then he invited the gentleman to stretch out his hand, and when he did, it was completely restored. And the Pharisees went out to join the Herodians to find a way to kill the insolent Nazarene.

It is enlightening to see how a hard heart reacts. The Pharisees are not asking how Jesus was able to heal a hand. That was inconsequential. They were not asking if the man needed his hand healed. They were not standing in line to congratulate him on his good fortune. The rules had been broken; that burned in their minds as a match can brown an autumn leaf.

But then what was Christ to do? Was he to avoid offending the Pharisees and help perpetuate this farce? Was he to acquiesce to absurdity? Fortunately for us his actions have not left us to wonder.

It has often been said that Jesus healed people to prove he was the Christ. Doubtless this is true, but if that is all we understand about his miracles, we miss their depth. Christ also healed because he loved people. He was moved by their infirmities.

He refused to be stifled by religious mummies at the cost of putting off people in need. He loved a woman whose back was bent over like a taco shell. He loved a man who had never seen a child's laughing eyes. The Pharisees loved laws that would not shake or bend. For Christ the choice was easy.

Certainly Christ could have waited. Sunday would have been an equally good day to heal someone. Some of the people Jesus healed he had seen often, so one must assume that he had a motive for pressing the day. He wanted to accomplish a package deal. Demonstrate that he was the Messiah, help some hurting people, and throw a monkey wrench into the whole stiff, heartless mentality.

It is obvious that Jesus had a broader concept of righteousness than his objectors. For instance, in one of his encounters over the Sabbath he reminded them that they thought it permissible to circumcise a child on the eighth day (Lev. 12:3), and when that day fell on the Sabbath, they merely proceeded with the process.

When two laws collided, they made adjustments and went on with life. What, then, should happen when healing and the Sabbath cross paths? Is circumcision more righteous than helping the needy? Their answer to that question would shed a lot of light on their concept of God and man.

Lenski summarizes the lessons for us very well.

"The argument is thus quite simple: on the one hand, a beneficial act involving one member; on the other hand, a beneficial act involving the entire body. The force of the argument, however, is increased in two ways. Whereas Moses commands circumcision also on the Sabbath, these Jews will not so much as permit a healing on the Sabbath. The conferring of a benefit means so much to Moses that he will not let even the Sabbath stand in the way; the conferring of a benefit means so little to the Jews that they misuse the Sabbath and force it to stand in the way." [3]

While justice may be blind, it is not cold-hearted. It understands mitigating circumstances. The laws of compassion are the greatest laws of compulsion.

The moral policeman has learned how to direct traffic, but he has never learned to really care. No place is this more glaring than when they ask Jesus about divorce.

If Jesus thought he had trouble explaining divorce to his antagonists, let him try explaining it today. No matter what he says about it, there will be some churches that will bar him from their pulpits. Indeed, carloads of church members will castigate him for even discussing such a controversial subject. Having tried to teach the subject to the twentieth-century church, he may choose to go back and face the original Pharisees.

A young man was being interrogated by a crowd of ministers in preparation for ordination. After the usual battery of questions one man arose and asked the candidate to

3. R. C. H. Lenski, *The Interpretation of John's Gospel* (Minneapolis: Augsburg Publishing House, 1961), p. 554.

outline his position on divorce. The novice said, "Gentlemen, I would rather not reply to that question. I know that whatever answer I give, at least one-third of the group will become upset." The issue was not pursued, and no one arose to deny the truth of the statement.

This is only part of the problem of having everything prepackaged. Inflexibility is the first cousin to unteachability.

Christ's views on divorce would really be of small significance to our immediate theme except for the reason why he addressed the subject. Matthew tells us that the Pharisees had spread a net to attempt to ensnare Jesus (19:3). The same word for *test* is used in Matthew, chapter four to describe the motives of Satan. Their ambition was not clarification but character assassination.

They attempt similar plots on other occasions, such as their questions concerning paying taxes to Caesar. First-century Judaism was split into at least three divisions on the problem, and as usual all parties were volatile.

The challenge was to attempt to interpret Deut. 24:1: "When a man hath taken a wife, and married her, and it come to pass that she find no favour in his eyes, because he hath found some uncleanness in her: then let him write her a bill of divorcement, and give it in her hand, and send her out of the house" (KJ).

What constitutes "some uncleanness"? The following gentlemen represented the prevailing views:

The Shammaites said it meant sexual unfaithfulness. Usually a strict interpreter, Shammai saw no other justifiable grounds for divorce.

The Hillelites said it meant that anything the husband did not like about his wife constituted sufficient grounds. Hence, Hillel said a husband could divorce his wife "even if she spoiled his soup." Some feel that he was using that as a figure of speech, but only Hillel could say that for sure.

Usually Hillel was a great defender of human rights and normally leaned toward compassion. In fact he had popularized the negative form of the Golden Rule before Jesus gave the positive version. However, when it came to marriage, he gave absolute authority to the husband. Possibly he felt that such power caused the women to work harder for harmony.

Aqiba managed to outdo Hillel. He maintained that a man could divorce his wife if he found a prettier woman.[4] She didn't even have to burn the soup. Nevertheless, he may have considered himself strict since he insisted that every cent of the marriage-contract money be paid to the dismissed spouse.

With laws on divorce this open, it would be easy to assume that divorce must have been rampant in Israel. This was evidently far from the case. As one writer has suggested, Jewish marriages were not looking for reasons to get divorced. Their background, their training, their mutual respect, their relatives, and their sense of moral duty committed them to a lifelong marriage. The average Hebrew wife did not worry daily that she might scorch the wheat cakes and end up out on the street. They may not have wanted for a law to divorce, but great multitudes of them wanted for a reason.[5] There were simply a lot of happy Jewish families.

Maybe it says something to our society. Possibly we do not need stronger laws but only happier people.

The question is, does Jesus want to stick his hand in this hornet's nest? If he does, he cannot avoid being stung. If one hornet caresses him, another will nail him.

It becomes very educational that Christ does not duck the issue. He could have excused himself and said, "I have a more important ministry of evangelism," or, "These are local matters. I am concerned about the kingdom."

4. Neusner, op. cit., p. 114.
5. Abrahams, op. cit., p. 78.

Jesus explained what God's intentions were. God did not want anyone to get divorced because he created man and woman to live together. However, Moses realized that if a mate was sexually unfaithful, the couple probably would not continue to live together. Their inability to forgive and reconcile would possibly cause insurmountable difficulties. Consequently, because of the "hardness" of peoples' hearts, God allowed divorce, and Moses wrote it into law. Jesus defended that system, though not ideal, to be just and fair.

He stated that if people divorced for any other reason and remarried, they committed adultery. That summary pleased a lot of people and caught in the craw of a lot of others.

Having stated that position, Jesus did not go on to try to clarify every facet, which Christians have since contrived. Can a divorced and remarried couple join a local church? Can a divorcee teach Sunday school? If the husband commits adultery and remarries, can the former wife remarry? It would have been so much easier if Jesus had only added a few more paragraphs.

Would it be unfair to suggest that he did not discuss these matters because he did not consider them important? But they are vital to many twentieth-century Christians. They are grounds for firing ministers, splitting churches, and expelling members. Doesn't it seem peculiar that Christ ignored some problems that are vital to some of his followers? Surely that must tell us something.

It is not uncommon to have a modern minister nit-picking with two divorcees who want to get married to each other. He looks at the gentleman and says, "Are you sure your former wife committed adultery?" "Well, have you had sexual relations since?" "But your wife did it first . . ." "Boy, that's good."

Our conscience should scream out—*people* not brittle laws. Let's talk about forgiveness, repentance, reconciliations, love, tomorrow, and God. Take the moral policemen off their beats and try to help rather than condemn. Adultery is wrong—now let us help the adulterer.

The laws of God are essential, but those laws are sensitive and caring, rather than cold and concrete. One of those laws says this, "He has enabled us to be ministers of a new covenant—not of the letter but of the Spirit; for the letter kills, but the Spirit gives life" (2 Cor. 3:6). And again Paul wrote, "But now, by dying to what once bound us, we have been released from the law so that we serve in a new way of the Spirit, and not in the old way of the written code" (Rom. 7:6).

The bill of divorcement was a very uncomplicated affair. Neither lawyers nor courts were necessary. No one had to prove the charges. All the husband would have to do was write a couple of sentences on a piece of paper, hand it to his wife, and show her the door.

If it was to the husband's advantage, he could make a public issue out of it and even call in witnesses. He might do this to protect his reputation or to quiet some of her relatives. Sometimes he might choose to do it privately, as Joseph had planned for Mary.

Under practically no circumstance could a wife divorce her husband.

To further appreciate what Christ has said on the subject we need to realize his contribution to womanhood. The Old Testament appeared to give value to the husband and treat the wife as a chattel. He explained that, despite popular views, this was not true. For those husbands who were prone to capriciously dispose of their spouses, Jesus reminded them that God never sanctioned such behavior. In doing so, he defended the equal value of women.

Many groups of Christians have felt that if the church is not very strong against divorce, we will not be able to stem the present tide. Maybe we need to learn a lesson from the ancient Jews. Strong ecclesiastical laws may prevent the fact of divorce. They cannot stop infidelity, they cannot stop fist fights, they cannot force two people to look into each other's eyes and say, "I love you."

We have grabbed the moral code by the wrong end. We don't want the horse to trounce on the tomatoes so we grip his tail and try to hold him back. How long would it take before we learn to lead him through?

Maybe Abrahams is correct when he says that Jewish families stayed together not because they had to but because they wanted to. Let the moral policemen turn in their badges and become teachers of the basic principles of God-led contentment.

Questions for Further Thought

1. What do you consider to be the role of the minister in relationship to your morality?

2. Why did the Pharisees object to the picking of grain?

3. What did Jesus mean—"The Son of man is Lord of the Sabbath"?

4. Why didn't Jesus wait until Sunday to heal the shriveled hand?

5. Do you feel that your local church is too lenient or too strict?

6. What will happen to the church if it liberalizes its local laws?

7. Do you see your role as a moral policeman? Is this your church's role?

Bibliography

Abrahams, Israel. *Studies in Pharisaism and the Gospels*, Library of Biblical Studies, edited by Harry Orlinsky. New York: KTAV Publishing House, Inc., 1967.

Adler, Morris. *The World of the Talmud*. New York: Schocken Books, 1966.

Ausubel, Nathan. *The Book of Jewish Knowledge*. New York: Crown Publishers, Inc.

Baeck, Leo. *The Pharisees and Other Essays*. New York: Schocken Books, 1947.

Barclay, William. *The Gospel of Matthew*. Philadelphia: The Westminister Press, 1958.

Bonhoeffer, Dietrich. *The Cost of Discipleship*. New York: The Macmillan Co., 1973.

Bright, John. *A History of Israel*, 2d ed. Philadelphia: Westminister Press, 1972.

Bruce, F. F. *Biblical Exegesis in the Qumran Texts*. Grand Rapids, Mich.: Wm. B. Eerdmans Publishing Co., 1959.

_____. *The Book of Acts*. Grand Rapids, Mich.: Wm. B. Eerdmans Publishing Co., 1960.

_____. *Israel and the Nations*. Grand Rapids, Mich.: Wm. B. Eerdmans Publishing Co., 1963

Buttrick, George A., ed. *The Interpreter's Dictionary of the Bible.* 4 vols. Nashville, Tenn.: Abingdon Press, 1962.

Edersheim, Alfred. *Sketches of Jewish Social Life.* Grand Rapids, Mich.: Wm. B. Eerdmans Publishing Co., 1964.

————. *The Life and Times of Jesus the Messiah.* Grand Rapids, Mich.: Wm. B. Eerdmans Publishing Co., 1971.

Geldenhuys, Norval. *Commentary on the Gospel of Luke,* The New International Commentary on the New Testament, edited by F. F. Bruce. Grand Rapdis, Mich.: Wm. B. Eerdmans Publishing Co., 1963.

Hallesby, O. *Prayer.* Minneapolis: Augsburg Publishing House, 1936.

Henry, Carl F. H. *Christian Personal Ethics.* Grand Rapids, Mich.: Wm. B. Eerdmans Publishing Co., 1957.

Herford, R. Travers. *Talmud and Apocrypha.* New York: KTAV Publishing House, Inc., 1971.

Hiebert, D. Edmond. *Mark, A Portrait of the Servant.* Chicago: Moody Press, 1974.

Howie, Carl G. *The Creative Era.* Richmond, Va.: John Knox Press, 1965.

Jeremias, Joachim. *Jerusalem in the Time of Jesus.* Philadelphia: Fortress Press, 1969.

Josephus. *Antiquities.* Translated by William Whiston. Grand Rapids, Mich.: Kregel Publications, 1969.

Lenski, R. C. H. *The Interpretation of John's Gospel.* Minneapolis: Augsburg Publishing House, 1961.

————. *The Interpretation of St. Matthew's Gospel.* Columbus, Ohio: The Wartburg Press, 1951.

Moe, Olaf. *The Apostle Paul.* Grand Rapids, Mich.: Baker Book House, 1954.

Moore, George Foot. *Judaism.* Vol. 1. Cambridge, Mass.: Harvard University Press, 1966.

Neusner, Jacob. *From Politics to Piety.* Englewood Cliffs, N.J.: Prentice-Hall, Inc., 1973.

Pfeiffer, Charles F. *Between the Testaments*. Grand Rapids, Mich.: Baker Book House, 1959.

Riggs, James Stevenson. *A History of the Jewish People*. New York: Charles Scribner's Sons, 1906.

Robertson, A. T. *Word Pictures in the New Testament*. 6 vols. Nashville, Tenn.: Broadman Press, 1930.

Runes, Dagobert D., ed. *Concise Dictionary of Judaism*. New York: Philosophical Library, 1959.

Schürer, Emil. *A History of the Jewish People in the Time of Jesus Christ*. Vol. 2. Div. 2. New York: Charles Scribner's Sons, 1896.

Singer, Isidor, ed. *The Jewish Encyclopedia*. Vol. 9. New York: KTAV Publishing House, Inc., n.d.

Tournier, Paul. *The Person Reborn*. New York: Harper and Row, Publishers, 1966.

Unger, Merrill F. *Unger's Bible Dictionary*. Chicago: Moody Press, 1960.

Vine, W. E. *An Expository Dictionary of New Testament Words*. London: Oliphants Ltd., 1959.

Index

Talmud, 73
Talmud, B. K., 48
Talmud and Apocrypha (Herford), 96
Tax collectors, 46–50, 97, 101, 121
  Pharisees and, 48, 50
Tefillin, 117
Tithing, 72–74, 75
Tolerance, 91, 97
Torah, 118, 122
Tournier, Dr. Paul, 90, 120
Tradition, 78–79

Uncleanness, 133–134
Unger, Merrill F., 63
Unger's Bible Dictionary, 63
Universal priesthood of believers, doctrine of, 88–89

Vine, W. E., 77

Wars (Josephus), 84

Washing of hands, 11
Water, cleansing by, 42–43
Webster's New Collegiate Dictionary, 24
Whiston, William, 21, 84, 109
Widows, 58–60, 61
Wilkerson, Dave, 66
William the Conqueror, 107
Women, 14, 133-136
Word Pictures in the New Testament (Robertson), 49
World of the Talmud, The (Adler), 10
World War II, 47, 105

Xenophobia, 121

Zacchaeus, 46, 47, 50
Zechariah, 37
Zeus, 20
Zionism, 99

Other Books by
William Coleman
from Bethany House Publishers

Counting Stars
The Good Night Book
The Great Date Wait and Other Hazards
Listen to the Animals
More About My Magnificent Machine
My Hospital Book
My Magnificent Machine
On Your Mark
Singing Penguins and Puffed-Up Toads
Today I Feel Like a Warm Fuzzy
Today I Feel Loved
Chesapeake Charlie and the Bay Bank Robbers
Chesapeake Charlie and Blackbeard's Treasure
Chesapeake Charlie and the Stolen Diamond